Crossing the Jordan River

About the Cover Art

Coexistence Or?...

Being an Israeli who has lived for 6 years in two Arab countries I have been exposed to different cultures and landscapes. With the recent unrest in the Middle East it seems that violent forces are pulling apart the core of coexistence of the nations in the region. Having been an active part of peace making I am disturbed and concerned.

With these 3 panels (burlap, kaffiyah sewn on canvas, 30" x 20") I mean to draw attention to both the physical size of the land and its layout.

Different fabrics have been sewn on 3 canvas panels. A red and white Kafia(traditional Arab headdress) depicts the Arab States surrounding Israel: Syria and Lebanon in the north, Jordan east and Egypt in the south. The Mediterranean is on the left.

Fraying at the edges. Israel is depicted in sackcloth representing the suffering of its people, as described in the Old Testament, the book of Esther 4,3: "There was great mourning among the Jews and fasting and weeping and wailing and many lay in sackcloth and ashes."

The third panel is a vision of what could happen if we shall not find a way to live together. So we would be left only with remnants.

Annette Rosen

Crossing the Jordan River

The Journeys of an Israeli Diplomat

Jacob Rosen

Humanics Trade Group
Atlanta, GA USA

Crossing the Jordan River
A Humanics Trade Group Publication

First Edition

Humanics Trade Group Publications is an imprint of and published by Humanics Publishing Group, a division of Brumby Holdings, Inc. Its trademark, consisting of the words "Humanics Trade Group" and the portrayal of a pegasus, is registered in the U.S. Patent and Trademark Office and in other countries.

Brumby Holdings, Inc.
1197 Peachtree St.
Suite 533B
Atlanta, GA 30361
USA

Printed in the United States of America and the United Kingdom

ISBN (Paperback) 0-89334-387-0
ISBN (Hardcover) 0-89334-388-9

Library of Congress Control Number: 2003103530

To the many residents of Amman who, with their warm hospitality, opened their homes to us, and their hearts.

ACKNOWLEDGEMENTS

Many people took part in the conception of this book either as silent participants or patient listeners. Others were much more involved. First are my wife Annette and our three children Etai, Rinat and Nadav who dutifully schlepped with me from Cairo and New Delhi via Jerusalem to Amman and are part of the story. Ann Serwitz who retyped most of the chapters and reintroduced me to the rules of English grammar. There is a Polish popular proverb claiming that sometimes even a blind chicken may find a seed. Well, this happened to me when I was invited to the annual dinner of the Atlanta Press Club in 2002 by its executive director Amal Morcos. She seated me around the same table with Gary Wilson and Larry Lowenstein and I discovered that Gary owns the Humanics Publishing Group and Larry is his long time advisor and guru. From then onwards things accelerated. Chris Walker was appointed by them to be my editor and accepted me as I am. Gracias.

Two long time friends of us, Prof. Ken Stein and Prof. Dale Eickelman, saw what I was doing and nodded gently. This was the best indirect encouragement I ever got. I hope that my reading was correct.

Jerusalem, October 2003

INTRODUCTION

My family and I were privileged to live openly as Israelis, both in Cairo (1987-1989) and Amman (1994-2000). It was a fascinating and illuminating experience. We learned a great deal about Egyptian and Jordanian societies and also about ourselves as Israelis.

Time and again, we witnessed how we do not understand each other. When I say "we," I mean not only "we, the Israelis," but also the Europeans and Americans, who, like us, have gone through similar experiences.

Amman offered an extra bonus because of its significant Palestinian population: that of getting acquainted with Palestinians who were not living under Israeli rule. Our encounters with this group offered a different dimension. We were also lucky to meet a very interesting and vibrant group—Palestinians who were born and educated in Kuwait, and who were forced to leave following the recovery of that country from the Iraqi yoke in 1991.

The vignettes assembled in this booklet are based on real events. Each of these stands on its own merit and may be read at random and not in a particular order or sequence. The approach is anthropological, rather than political.

It is my hope that in sharing these stories with you, the readers, our experiences will somehow illustrate why and how the Arabs and the Israelis (and perhaps the West) fail to understand one another. They also show that after all is said and done, we are human beings who share the same concerns and inspirations. I hope that it will be a modest marker towards a better future.

Contents

A Car Called Mercedes

The German-made Mercedes is a symbol of status and power and is idolized in many Third World countries. Owning a Mercedes symbolizes one's status as being a part of the "inner circle."

My first diplomatic service post was in The Hague, Netherlands, and one of the first things I noticed was that while the diplomats from Western developed countries drove European or American-made cars, it seemed that all the diplomats from Third World countries drove a big black Mercedes. While in Egypt, we heard about Egyptian journalists who would receive a Mercedes from Saddam Hussein when they wrote positive stories about him. Jordan is not an exception to this Mercedes phenomenon. King Hussein used to grant a Mercedes to veteran officers, politicians, and Bedouin Chiefs.

There are many jokes and stories in Jordan about the Mercedes Culture, since many realize that it is not exactly a proper practice. Here is a one such story.

One day, the English Language Inspector in the Ministry of Education decided to visit the boys' school in the city of Al-Karak. The English teacher was very nervous and he was especially worried about one of his students. This student's father was a high-ranking military officer, but the student himself was not very clever. The teacher instructed this student to keep silent and not to raise his hand when the Inspector asked questions.

When the Inspector came to the class, he asked the students, in Arabic, "How do you say 'car' in English?" No one knew, and the only student who raised his hand was that unclever boy. The teacher was horrified and indicated to the student to put down his hand, but the boy persisted. The teacher pressed a finger to his throat indicating that he would kill the boy if he did not lower his hand. The Inspector, however, noticed that the boy had raised his hand and wanted to answer the question. The boy, in full confidence, replied, "Mercerdes, Sir."

The Casino in Jericho

For the most part, gambling is illegal in the Middle East. But in the U.S.A. and Europe gambling is a big industry, as people enjoy gambling and casinos. Israelis and Arabs are not different.

Israelis, for example, flock to Turkey (a secular Muslim democracy) where it is legal to gamble. When Egypt saw this potential financial windfall, it wanted to tap the Israeli gambling habit. So the Egyptian government established casinos at the Marriott Hotel in Cairo and at the Hilton Hotel in Taba on the Sinai peninsula. Holders of foreign passports were allowed in, but all Egyptians were barred.

When the Palestinian Authority was established it needed cash, and so they built a casino in Jericho, which is the oldest city in the world (6,000 years). Israelis by the thousands flocked there to gamble. Anyone was welcomed in the Jericho casino, except for Palestinians themselves.

After the opening of the Israeli Embassy in Amman, we started getting inquiries from Jordanians as to whether it would be possible for their Gulf State partners or friends to get a visa to Israel, either for business or "to pray at Al-Aqsa Mosque in Jerusalem" (Jerusalem being the 3rd holiest city in Islam).

Our policy was that Jerusalem was open to every believer. And since we did not have a quarrel with any Arab individuals from those States, we would usually grant them a visa, provided that they would go through a security procedure, prove that they had money, and convince us that they were bona fide travelers and were planning to return to Jordan.

After 1997, we started getting telephone calls from Saudis, asking to talk with the Ambassador or myself, inquiring as to whether they would be able to get a visa to "pray in Al-Aqsa Mosque." We assured them that, in principle, it could be done, provided that their names were not on some "black list."

The Saudis would then ask whether we could place their visas outside of their passports (to "hide" from their authorities that they had visited the enemy's country), to which we responded positively. They would then sometimes ask whether or not they could drive their own cars, and we responded that it would be more practical if they drove a car with Jordanian plates.

And, then, as it happened several times, came the ultimate question, "*Is the Al-Aqsa far from Jericho?*"

A COMMUNITY-FRIENDLY PROJECT

American entrepreneurs are people of vision. They "have it." They plan well, market well, and raise capital well. They are also "trend savvy" and are able to label and design a project which will address the latest "in" thing or concern. The American entrepreneurial spirit works in Palm Springs; it works in Europe; it should work in the Middle East as well. Does it?

A group of American and Israeli entrepreneurs had a vision to establish a huge international convention center with a theme water park on an artificial lagoon between Eilat and Aqaba on the Red Sea shore. Among other marvels, it was supposed to offer a casino (which both Israeli and Jordanian laws do not permit, at the moment).

True to the spirit of the newly forged peace between Jordan and Israel, the plan was to have the center be accessible from both Jordan and Israel through a special regime designed for that purpose. It got an initial, though not official, approval from the Israeli side. The Jordanian side gave a sort of optimistic indication that they would also be interested because of the huge tourism and employment potential which the project promised. Of course such an indication was not sufficient, and, at a certain point, the group of American entrepreneurs came to Amman to present the project to the Jordanian Authorities.

The main thrust of the presentation was that it was a multi-billion dollar project, which would provide thousands of jobs in the Aqaba region. Aqaba itself is the only port city of Jordan, the main gate for its imports and exports. The population of the city is composed mainly of hard-working citizens and only partly of people who work in tourism-related jobs. Most of the city's people are traditional. Men wearing Bedouin or Islamic gowns (*jallabiyyah*) are not a rare site in Aqaba. It goes without saying that most of the women wear traditional dress and their heads are covered.

The Jordanian ministers were quite overwhelmed by the American introduction, particularly by its scope. It threatened to totally change the labor scene of Aqaba, and perhaps, divert almost every laborer in the town from harbor services to that project.

One American partner forecasted that the project would employ 5,000 people. The Jordanians started asking questions, which indicated disbelief, skepticism, and, to my trained ear, a basic rejection, mainly because of the fear of changing the whole labor market in the city. The Americans are experienced marketing experts, and, noticing the initial hesitation, they tried to convince the Jordanians that the project would be "good, very good, for Jordan," because of the jobs and plentiful tourism potential. When these arguments didn't impress, the Americans pulled the ever-winning American card: "It will be a community-friendly project," which meant that the residents of Aqaba would have a special or easy access to the water park facilities.

What the entrepreneurs didn't know is that that is the ultimate nightmare in a traditional Muslim society—exposing the youth of both sexes to water parks and public beaches, where Western females in bikinis can be seen together with members of the opposite sex.

Women in the Arab world enter the water on the beach or a swimming pool dressed completely in their normal clothes. The "community-friendly project" has, thus far, never gotten off the ground.

A FEMALE BUNKER BUSTER

Neighbors watch each other, imitate each other, and, sometimes, even alter or reverse their own conduct because of the winds of change blowing from the other side. The holiest feast in Islam is the month of *Ramadan*, in which Muslims fast from dawn to dusk. They break the fast at the appearance of three stars in the sky and celebrate into the wee hours of the night, normally in big family gatherings and circles of friends.

The breaking of the fast (*Iftar*) offers a convenient political platform for the authorities to implement their agenda. Normally, it takes the form of the Head of State or his top ministers hosting *Iftar* parties for a selected groups of guests. Unlike family *Iftars*, which are mixed (men and women together), the official *Iftars* are segregated. Thus a Prime Minister will invite men for *Iftar*, and his spouse may host, in a separate location, an *Iftar* for women.

After the establishment of relations between Jordan and Israel, King Hussein began inviting Israeli Arabs to *Iftar*. It was an interesting event, since the guest list was arbitrary in nature: Muslim and Christian clergy, mayors, heads of local councils,

Circassians, Christians and even Druze. The guest list would also sometimes include Arab Members of Knesset (the Israeli Parliament) and representatives of the Israeli Embassy in Amman. All the invitees were, of course, males.

This tradition continued after King Hussein's death in 1999. The next year, King Abdallah held an *Iftar* party for a delegation of Israeli Arabs. The list of invitees was the same in nature as in previous years and included all the Arab (or rather all the non-Jewish) members of Knesset. Well, this is not exactly so, because in the General Elections in 1999, an Arab woman, Husniyyah Jabbarah, was elected for the first time to the Israeli Parliament. Since the invitations were personal and for men only, the new female MK was not invited. The interesting thing about Husniyyah Jabbarah is that she was a member of a Zionist Left wing party (*Meretz*) and not a member of an Arab Party.

Winds of change started blowing fast. Modern and outspoken in her approach, she started raising hell about her exclusion from the "Royal Party." The Israeli media watched this episode with great interest. The Royal Palace was quick in grasping the implications and reacted promptly. Husniyyah Jabbarah, the first Arab women in the Israeli Parliament, was extended an invitation, as was Mrs. Nadia Hilu, a Christian Arab from Jaffa, who narrowly missed her seat in the Knesset on the Labor Party ticket, and the veteran Arab Affairs correspondent of the Israeli Daily *Yediot Aharonot*, Smadar Peri, who is Jewish.

King Abdullah, in a royal gesture, invited the ladies to be seated beside him. And me? Well, I shared a table with amazed Jordanian male senators.

A JEWISH BRAIN

Societies in conflict tend to develop very strange and twisted images of each other. There are many terms to describe it; from mirror images to mutual demonization. The Arab-Israeli conflict has not escaped this lot.

The very anti-Semitic text, *The Protocols of the Elders of Zion*, is sold in almost every bookshop or street kiosk in both Egypt and Jordan, and I presume that it is probably the same in other Arab countries as well. Through my years in Amman, I realized that many Arabs do in fact believe that the Jews have a different mind, and some even presume that their brains are structured in a different way.

One day our daughter, Rinat, was playing soccer at school and somehow collided with another girl and fell hard on the ground. The school called us and suggested that we come and take her home. We called our doctor, who asked that we take her to a hospital to have an MRI to make sure that everything was fine. So we went to the hospital and entered the MRI section.

I was curious to see how it worked and asked the technician if I could be with him in his control room to watch the monitor. He was kind enough to agree. As is usual and customary in Arab countries, he asked me politely where we came from (I think this custom has origins in the tribal/nomadic traditions). The Arabs will ask for your name only a while after the conversation is in progress. Since every member of the staff in the hospital wore a badge with his or her name, I recognized from his surname that he was of a Palestinian origin. I replied tactfully that we are from "a neighboring country." He didn't get the point, so I elaborated that we are from "a neighboring country *not* from a sisterly country" (all Arabs States regard themselves Sisterly or Brotherly).

This time he got the point and understood very well. At this stage, the scan was in progress and images of Rinat's brain started showing up on the technician's monitor. He was taking a professional look at the screen, while simultaneously digesting the fact that he was in his cubical with an Israeli. I found it both funny and stimulating—a Palestinian technician and an Israeli diplomat watching a brain on a monitor.

I pointed my finger at the monitor and told him, "*Shuf, shuf, mukh Yahudi*"(Look, look, a Jewish brain!).

It took him a moment to understand the absurdity of the concept, and then he started rolling with laughter. So did I.

THE ALLENBY BRIDGE - THE KOREAN WAY

The oldest border crossing between Jordan and the West Bank is The Allenby Bridge, east of Jericho. It is named after General Allenby, the Commander of the British Forces who pushed away the Ottoman Army from Palestine in 1917/18. Like any other thing in our troubled historical region, the bridge has many different names given by different parties.

The Jordanians named this bridge after King Hussein Bin Talal (1936-1999). The Palestinians call the bridge Al-Karameh Crossing, to commemorate the unsuccessful 1968 Israeli incursion into a neighboring village of the same name on the east bank of the Jordan River. Yasser Arafat escaped from this incursion on a motorbike, and the Jordanian Army inflicted heavy losses on the Israelis.

In 1994 two more crossings, this time with all the legal international titles, were opened between Israel and Jordan: a northern crossing near Beth Shean on the Israeli side which the Jordanians named Sheikh Hussein Crossing (after the small village which is situated on its flanks), and the Arava Crossing, between Aqaba and Eilat on the Red Sea. One could imagine what confusion occurred in distinguishing between the King Hussein Bridge and Sheikh Hussein Bridge.

One day, I was invited to the home of our Political Counselor, Avivah Raz-Schechter. Among the other guests was a Korean regional representative of his home company. He resided in Amman but traveled throughout the entire region.

Since most Arab States will refuse entry to anyone who has an Israeli visa in his passport, many people have asked us if they could travel to Israel without the visa being stamped inside their passport. Our policy was quite practical and flexible. While not willing to become the leper or the outcast of the neighborhood, we tried to find a way to satisfy our national pride without swallowing it. In most cases, we would ask the person to write a letter explaining that he wanted to travel to Israel without hampering his chances to travel to other Arab countries. The Arabs, by the way, also became very creative in such cases when they wanted to admit holders of Israeli visas or even holders of Israeli passports.

The Korean asked me whether I could fix it for him to not have his visa stamped in his passport. I gave him my business card and asked him to write me a letter, including the dates of his desired visit and through which crossing he wished to pass. The next morning, I got a fax from him thanking me for my readiness to assist him in visiting Israel "via the *RNB Bridge*"!

AMBASSADORIAL ENVY

Ambassadors are, supposedly, perfect gentlemen. They are polite, understanding, smiling, never say "no," etc. In other words, they are any other man's ideal. Even military officers or hard working politicians, who usually scold, hold in contempt, and despise diplomats, usually have hidden ambitions to become Ambassadors. Once offered such a privilege, they fall in love with their new position, finding it difficult to ever give it up.

I arrived in Amman in December 1994 as *chargé d'affaires* for one month, with the mission of opening the Israeli Embassy there. By the terms of the Peace Agreement, an Ambassadorial exchange was supposed to take place one month later. Since that was the case, and since we had a lot of administrative and functional tasks to perform, I thought it would be a waste of time to pay courtesy visits to all the other Ambassadors in Amman. In any case, the "real" Ambassador, who would present his credentials to the King, was "on his way." Instead, I decided to concentrate on the # 2's in the major embassies, to establish working relations with my temporary counterparts.

Consequently, I made appointments in all the relevant embassies and showed up for the meetings. Much to my surprise, in most cases, I was received at the entrance by a secretary or an assistant, who took me to the # 2's room. There I was informed, shyly, by my host, that the meeting will be with His Excellency, the Ambassador, himself.

"You see, when my Ambassador heard that you were coming, he insisted on greeting you himself." Of course, I understood.

Imagine the eyebrows which would have been raised in different capitals when a report would have reached them about a meeting with the new Israeli *chargé d'affaires* in Amman, and it was filed by the # 2, and not the Ambassador himself. Ambassadors are, as previously noted, perfect gentlemen. They can also be envious.

AMERICAN JEWS VISIT KING HUSSEIN (OR A.S.T VS. M.E.S.T.*)

One of the meaningful triumphs of Jordanian diplomacy was its ability to establish a dialogue with the major Jewish organizations in the United States long before there was talk about a peace agreement between Jordan and Israel. Leaders of major American (and sometimes British) Jewish organizations visited Amman regularly and were welcomed in the Royal Palace.

After the Peace Agreement was signed and the Israeli Embassy was opened in Amman, many American Jewish organizations who regularly sent delegations to Israel added Jordan to their itineraries. Coming from Israel, they would spend a day in Petra (a Nabatean city sculptured in red rock) and then half of a day in Amman, which was to be dedicated mainly to a meeting with His Majesty, King Hussein. Sometimes they would also meet with the Prime Minister or the Minister of Foreign Affairs. How were such meetings arranged?

Normally, the American Jewish organizations would contact the Jordanian Ambassador in Washington, D.C. and request such meetings. Most of the time these meetings were arranged and confirmed in principle, though not with an exact time. The Jordanian Embassy would provide the head of the visiting group with a contact telephone number to call upon arrival in Amman.

Though it may seem strange, there is a logic in such an arrangement due to the nature of the Royal Palace's schedules and practices. Since the King had the privilege to stay with any visitors as long as he deemed necessary, it was difficult to stick to a rigid timetable. It happened many times that a group went to the Prime Minister's office for a meeting with him, just to be informed that His Majesty would see them at that exact moment. In such cases, the meeting with the Prime Minister would be re-scheduled, or the Prime Minister would join the group in the meeting with the King.

The Chiefs of Royal Protocol were very experienced and competent in switching meetings, even between Amman and Aqaba (flying the guests by choppers). It rarely happened that any meetings were cancelled.

All of this was fine for those familiar with the way things happened in Amman, but it was not so fine by American standards where they always follow timetables. After all, in America, time is money.

Needless to say, a scheduled meeting with His Majesty was a cause for excitement. In most cases, no contact was made with the U.S. State Department or the American Embassy in Amman, although the delegates of those organizations were U.S. citizens. The delegations were also strong supporters of the State of Israel, which normally would be the subject of the meetings. But the Israeli Embassy was also kept in the dark, and so, when the delegations began to arrive in Amman, they would call the contact number given to them in Washington. The number was usually that of the Protocol Division in the Ministry of Foreign Affairs or the Royal Palace.

The visitors would be politely advised to stay in the hotel and wait for a call from the Palace about the exact time of the meeting. And there is where the action began. Americans do not like spending time in a hotel waiting for a telephone call. After a while, they would call again just to hear the tranquilizing and polite advice to stay in the hotel and wait.

In most cases, group dynamics began to accelerate. Someone remembered that he was good friends with the U. S. Ambassador and called his office, which was surprised to learn that such a group was in town. The Ambassador politely repeated the advice to wait and promised that in the end, everything would fall into place.

Then someone suggested that they call the Israeli Embassy (sometimes the delegations actually stayed in the same hotel where the Embassy was located between 1994-1995). We were as surprised as the U. S. Embassy that such a delegation was in town. We added our accumulated experience and advice to wait for the call. We sensed an attitude of disappointment about our lack of ability to fix things.

The groups decided not to waste time and left the hotel for a short tour of the city. Naturally, while they were out, the Palace called. A nervous search was conducted by both the U.S. and Israeli Embassies to find the missing visitors.

To make a long story short: no one was lost. The King saw and charmed them all, and the Americans got a good lesson about Middle Eastern Standard Time.

*(American Standard Time vs. Middle Eastern Standard Time)

BEDOUIN OBSERVATION CAPABILITIES

The *Bedouins*, the "desert dwellers," are famous for their observation and tracking capabilities. The desert is vast and monotonous, and the Bedouins, who are masters of the desert, notice every slight change which occurs there. They are first-class pathfinders. Some of them even serve in the Israeli Defense Forces as pathfinders, and some have been killed in action, creating a strong blood bond with their Jewish brothers-in-arms.

In March, 1997, I was *chargé d'affaires* (Ambassador Oded Eran hadn't arrived yet), and we were expecting a visit from the Israeli Minister of Defense, Yitzhak Mordechai. Minister Mordechai, a native of Kurdistan, grew up in Project Gimel in Upper Tiberias (I grew up in Project Daled there). He was a retired general who served most of his life in the Paratrooper Corps. Because of that, the Jordanian hosts decided to demonstrate to him some commando/paratrooper exercises east of the city of Al-Zarqa, on the fringes of the desert.

Our security officer was instructed to make an exploratory tour of the area of the exercise, as is common practice in such cases. A young Jordanian Bedouin officer was assigned to explain to him whatever needed an explanation. This was the end of a very dry winter and a few days earlier there was a sudden, relatively bountiful rain. A delicate and thin layer of green covered the hills in the area. When our security officer arrived there with his Bedouin companion, the Bedouin remarked instinctively: "It's greener here."

The Bedouin mind and concern is geared initially to physical changes concerning water and grazing, since they wander and raise herds. A lack of water or grass will compel them to be on the move, which reminds me of another story I heard from Ambassador Moshe Sasson in this context:

One day, at the beginning of the 20th Century, the Chief of the Sheikhs of the Bedouin tribes in Beersheba was leading a meeting of the tribal chieftains in the area. They were sitting on the ground in a tent in a circle, while behind them, like back benchers, were sitting the younger Bedouins. These younger Bedouins were tacit observers or silent students following the discussion, but they had no right to interfere. Suddenly, while they were discussing tribal affairs, a messenger from Istanbul showed up with an imperial decree from the Sublime Port (The Sultan). He opened the rolled decree and presented it to the Chief of the Sheikhs. The Chief was illiterate and couldn't read, so he turned to the Sheikh on his left and asked him whether he could read. He was also illiterate. Turning to the one on his right yielded the same result. He turned to the rest of the Sheikhs, but all of them were illiterate.

Then, one of the young "back benchers" asked the Chief of the Sheikhs for permission to look at the decree. The Sheikh asked him whether he was literate and he answered "no," but added that nevertheless, he would like to have a look at it. The Chief of the Sheikhs handed him the decree. The young man looked at it, turning it over 90 degrees, then another 90, until he examined all 360 degrees. Then, he informed the Chief of the Sheikhs: "The number of the standing letters is bigger than the number of the sitting letters*, which means transfer" (an order to move from the present camping area).

*In the Arabic alphabet, there are vertical (standing) letters and horizontal (sitting) letters. In European alphabets, there are, also, vertical letters, such as b, d, f, h, k, l and t and horizontal letters, such as a, c, e, m, n, r, s, u, w, and x.

BIRDS RECOGNIZE NO BORDERS

One day, I got a call from the secretary of the American Community School in which our children studied. She asked me to help a fiancé of one of the school's assistant teachers. The fiancé had a pet shop in Amman and used to import Amazonian parrots to Jordan. He had a Dutch partner, who would fly them to Brussels and from there to Amman. The partner had three parrots ready to fly to Amman, when his travel agent informed him that the scheduled flight to Amman was cancelled.

He asked the travel agent what the alternatives were, and she replied that they had a flight from Brussels to Eilat, an Israeli city on the Red Sea and a favorite holiday resort for Northern Europeans. This city is located a mile from the border with Jordan and basically faces the City of Aqaba. She explained to her customer that since Eilat is so close to Jordan, it wouldn't be a problem to fly there and then take the parrots across the border.

Being Dutch, which means precise and organized (I know from personal experience since my wife is from the Netherlands), he was worried about the Israeli veterinary requirements. So, he called the Israeli Embassy in Brussels and asked whether there would be any problems for him in bringing the birds to Jordan via Israel (transit). The Israeli who answered his call inquired as to whether he had all the necessary documents, and he responded that he did. So the Israeli told him there would be no problem.

What the travel agent didn't tell the Dutch man was that since the airplane was of a heavier kind, it would not land in the Eilat Airport (which is in the midst of the city), but, instead, it would be diverted to an Israeli Air Force Base called *Ovdah*, which is located some twenty-five miles northwest of the city. In such cases, the Immigration and Customs people would travel to the airbase, process the passengers, and return to Eilat.

So, the Dutch partner, unaware of all this, landed safely in "Eilat," stepped down from the aircraft, picked up the cages and proceeded to Customs. The Customs Officical asked him about the birds and he answered that he was in transit with them, going to Jordan. He was asked to show the paperwork, only to discover that Israel was a signatory of the CITES (Convention on International Trade of Endangered Species) and that he did not possess the relevant documentation which allowed these parrots to be in his possession. Surprised, he asked what the alternatives were, only to be told that they would have to fly back to Brussels. He explained it was very impractical for a variety of reasons and added, in desperation, that the birds were not very healthy and needed medicine, etc.

The answer he got was: "So, we have to put them to sleep."

After a long period of bargaining, nervous telephone calls to the Nature Reserves Authority, the regional veterinary office, and others, they all agreed to keep them for two days in a neighboring nature reserve until he could produce the required documents.

Frustrated, he gave the birds to the Customs Officicals and, being Dutch (precise), he asked for a receipt stating that they had taken the birds from him. The answer he got was ludicrously funny. "We are sorry; this is a military airport, and we do not have forms for birds."

So the birds were left at the mercy of the Israeli system and he rushed on to Jordan. At that time, I got a telephone call from the school. I invited the Jordanian and his Dutch partner to the Embassy and heard their story. It seemed that only intervention with the head of the Israeli Veterinary Services would help.

So, I called the "Boss," Dr. Arnon Shimshoni, who studied veterinary medicine at the University of Utrecht in the Netherlands. To the amazement of the Dutch partner, I spoke to Dr. Shimshoni in Dutch. He understood the problem and referred me to the man in charge of quarantines in his office. I called and asked for a solution, due to the fact that the birds were just in transit and never intended to land in Israel.

The man who answered said that there might be a problem.

I asked "Why?" and he responded, "Because I am the man who gave the instruction not to let them in!"

Common sense prevailed, nevertheless. It took another hour of consultations, and the next day, the Dutch partner and his Jordanian colleague drove down to Aqaba, crossed the border, (we had to issue a quick visa for the Jordanian) and recovered the birds from the Nature Reserve, where they were hosted.

BUSINESS CARDS

We, the diplomats who move from place to place, have to develop means and ways to get acquainted with as many people as possible in a short time. Business cards are one of the tools to achieve this. Coming to a reception or a meeting, a diplomat will exchange as many cards as possible with other participants whose agenda is basically the same.

Normally, one engages in small talk, trying to estimate as quickly as possible whether the other conversant is interesting or just "one of those" who are there but are good for nothing. Most of the people, most of the time, are relevant but it doesn't always show, at least not immediately. Sometimes, one is engaged in a talk with a good potential, just to be interrupted by a spouse or another well-wishing person.

A diplomat, even a good diplomat, cannot always remember all the names, so the exchange of business cards for contact in the near future is very important. During the first meeting one tries to write a short remark on the card obtained to remind oneself of that person or some additional data received about him from another person.

When a diplomat is new, he carries in his pocket at least 20-30 of his own business cards and his yield should be the same in big events. People who are invited to such events, either businessmen, government officials, or members of the free professions, are familiar with the routine and, in most of the cases, will carry their own cards. Of course, it may happen, from time to time, that one runs out of cards but experienced people make sure that they have enough of them.

So, when I arrived in Amman, I followed this very familiar pattern. I was invited to functions and events, talked to people by my own initiative or was introduced by someone else, usually the host, who was proud to introduce the new Israeli *chargé d'affaires,* and was actively engaged in the art of business card exchange.

It worked as expected with the members of the diplomatic community, but I faced some unexpected difficulty with the Jordanians. Everyone was polite and no one turned his back on me; we even conversed in Arabic (at that stage I still had remnants of the Egyptian dialect in my Arabic, which I presume sounded strange coupled with my heavy Polish accent), but when the moment came to exchange cards, after I had pushed my own, the typical reaction was an apologetic sentence: "Oh, I'm sorry, I've left my cards in my other suit/shirt" or: "I'm sorry, I ran out of cards" or: "I'll fax you my card tomorrow." It was only at a much later stage, when I became well-acquainted with most of them, that they admitted they were very reluctant to give me their cards. They explained that they had no idea who I really was. An Israeli who speaks Arabic is most probably a *Mossad* (the Israeli C.I.A.) agent, they suspected. Only after a while, when they learned and verified who I really was, would they relax and open up.

All this long introduction is necessary background for the following story. In one of those receptions, I was introduced to a wealthy Jordanian businessman of Palestinian origin. He told me that he owned several gas stations in Amman and was also involved in "general import/export," which means that he tries his luck in any sort of commercial transaction which might produce some profit. I, of course, started with my own shtick/agenda, emphasizing that there was probably good potential for him to do business with Israel and suggested that he should visit Israel to see what he could import/export, or host an Israeli businessmen who could start coming to Jordan to find out what opportunities were there.

The conversation was nice, friendly, to the point, and we even joked. By the time we were "done," I handed him my business card and told him that I'd call him soon. He took my card, put it in his pocket and didn't offer me his card. He didn't apologize about forgetting his card. He just was ready to go.

Since we joked before, I asked him whether he was "one of those who forgot their cards it their other suit."

He looked at me and replied simply: "No, I do not carry business cards; I do not have business cards."

I was intrigued and told him: "You are a businessman. How do you do business without having cards?"

His response was not late in coming: "Mr. Rosen, I'm well-known in Amman. Everyone knows me. I do not need cards. You are new in town. You need cards."

By the way, after this repeated show of "forgetting my cards in my other suit," I started telling the Jordanians that I accept also credit cards. I added that I didn't need them for the credit, just for their name, which was printed on them.

CAN YOU FIX ME A MEETING WITH THE KING?

The Jewish people have a long history that goes back at least 3,500 years, from the days of Abraham in Mesopotamia, through the slavery in Egypt, the Exodus, the return to the Promised Land, the Kingdom of David and Solomon, then the Exile and Return, and so on. We used to have our Kings, some of them good and enlightened, some of them crooks and dictators. After losing independence following the destruction of the 2nd Temple in 70 A.D., we lived in exile for about 2 millennia. In all our prayers, we yearn and long to re-establish our Kings.

We already have our State, but so far no King. So what do Jews do in such a case? Like in a Jewish cooking book which starts with, "borrow an egg from a neighbor," we try to borrow them from the neighbors.

Despite the long history of conflict with Jordan, King Hussein managed to capture the sympathy and respect of many Israelis. It was probably his personality and humanity which made him so liked by the Israelis.

I can't think of any Israeli visitor to Jordan, whether official or private, senior or junior, who didn't express his wish, whether directly or indirectly, to have a chance to meet King Hussein.

I could fill pages about the different ways and means, which were employed to this end. For example, some Israeli Arabs boasted to their Jewish friends that they had contacts in the Royal Palace and could "fix it" for them; or we received calls from different Israeli Ministers' offices to the Embassy in Amman. In such calls, the Israeli Ministers assistants would inform us that their Minister would be delighted to honor us with a visit, provided that we fix him a visit to the Palace.

Once we participated in bilateral talks between senior officials. The negotiations were not easy and, at a certain moment, the leader of the Israeli delegation informed his Jordanian counterpart that he believed that if his Minister would meet His Majesty, King Hussein, the particular problem might be overcome.

The real problem surfaced when there was an invitation to a Minister or another high-ranking person to visit the Palace or to have lunch with His Majesty. Everyone wanted to join and we poor diplomats had to use our wits to keep the numbers correct, protocol-wise.

CONDOLENCES, ETIQUETTE, HONOR, TACT AND WISDOM

One of the most important pillars of the Arab society, if not the most prominent one, is honour. It has plenty of manifestations and is very central in all aspects of Arab life. A man or woman without the respect of his society and environment is an outcast, and life is senseless without honour. The smallest insult or gesture, negligible in the Western hemisphere, may become a very serious issue, which can easily catch momentum and turn into a feud involving whole clans and tribes. Thus, every effort is invested to avoid such gestures and it is no wonder that with time certain types of protocols were developed for this purpose.

Death is considered in the Arab society as the Lord's decision, which should be accepted without questioning or grievance. Condolences are offered for three days after the funeral with total separation between men and women.

Thus, women pay condolences to the deceased's women relatives, normally during the morning and early afternoon hours. Men pay condolences by the same manner to the male relatives during the late afternoon and evening hours in cases where the condolences are offered at the deceased's home.

Sometimes the condolences are offered to females and males in two different locations so that men and women can come throughout the whole day. Sometimes, if it is a big family and the house is big enough, the condolences are offered simultaneously for men and women, but in different parts of the house with separate entrances or in a special tent out in the yard. In some cases the condolences period may be extended for a whole week, thus enabling people from far away to arrive (which happens mainly among Bedouins).

An interesting episode happened during the paying of condolences to Ambassador Dr. Samir Mutawi', then Jordan's Ambassador to The Netherlands on the occasion of his father's death. Dr. Mutawi' studied and lived for a long time in the United Kingdom and the Netherlands, and wrote a very good book about Jordan during the 1967 war.

Since I knew him quite well, I went one afternoon to offer condolences for the death of his father (he died in Australia during a visit to one of his sons and the family had to fly his body to Amman and then via Allenby Bridge to the West Bank). As I entered, I realized that Zaid Al-Rifaí, Ex-Prime Minister and at that time the Speaker of the Jordanian Senate, was there. He was seated on one of the few comfortable armchairs, which are kept for V.I.P.s in such situations. Other people sit on normal iron or plastic chairs which are provided for occasions where hundreds of people turn out. Unless one is a close family member he or she is supposed to stay between 15-20 minutes, sip a cup of Arabic coffee, chat with other people about the deceased, politics, or even a light gossip. In many cases there is a member of the clergy, offering a prayer in memory of the deceased in intervals of about 15 minutes which is a sort of pacer and reminder to people that it is time to leave and not to stay until the next round of prayers.

So, Zaid Al-Rifaí, whose late father was also a Prime Minister several times, was there talking to people about the situation. Everyone was listening to what he was saying and of course no one would leave while he was talking. Leaving while such a respected person is talking means also turning your back to someone, something that should be avoided in Arab culture.

More people were coming and no one was leaving. Among the new arrivals was Dr. Abd Alsalam Al–Majali, also an Ex-Prime Minister (he is the one who actually signed the Peace Agreement with Israel in 1994). After serving as Prime Minister he became, as is the custom in Jordan, a Senator. Dr Al-Majali, a medical doctor who studied in the United Kingdom, was a General in the Jordanian Army and as such carries also the title *Basha* (a Turkish title for a general) and belongs to one of the most respected and influential East Jordanian families from Al-Karak in South Jordan.

This town produced several Prime Ministers including another one from the same family, Hazá Al-Majali, who was assassinated in 1960 and whose youngest son, Col. Hussein Al-Majali, was for many years the chief of security of the late King Hussein. By sheer coincidence or not Col. Hussein Al-Majali and Dr. Mutawi' are brothers-in-law since both are married to two Palestinian sisters from the Al–Masri family in Nablus.

So Dr. Al-Majali entered, greeted everybody and was directed by Dr. Mutawi' to another V.I.P. armchair. A very fascinating conversation developed between him and Zaid Al-

Rifaí. While noticing my presence they made reference to the Holy Land and Jerusalem. Zaid Al Rifaí, who studied once at Harvard and served as Jordan's Ambassador to London in the early Seventies, remarked that there is something magnetic in Jerusalem. "Anyone who wanted to become a prophet, be he Jewish, Christian or Muslim had to pass through Jerusalem and have it on his C.V." The intellectual and fascinating exchange between them continued, and of course more people came and no one was leaving. This is one of the virtues of the Arab Civility: respect, respect and again respect. No excuses of another appointment or previous commitment. You do not turn your back and leave before the dignitaries. It went on for about forty-five minutes, far beyond the condolences routine. Then, Zaid Al-Rifaí stood up intending to leave. The host, Dr. Mutawi' came immediately to his side to accompany him to the door.

And then the real "action" started. Dr.Abd Alsalam Al-Majali stood up as well intending to leave. Dr.Mutawi' maneuvered himself masterfully between the two of them accompanying them to the door. However, the door was not wide enough for both of them, and one had to give way to the other. Courtesy, Seniority, Importance, Symbolism and many other virtues and issues are embodied in the dilemma of who will step out first. It was clear that the more important should go out first. Who was more important, protocol-wise, the current Speaker of the Senate who served several times as a Prime Minister, Ambassador to the U.K., and Chief of the Royal Court, or Senator Al-Majali who also served several times as Prime Minister, was a General in the Army and belongs also to a very respected family?

I did not envy the host and the verdict he had to give. Neither man wanted to give up his seniority, but also neither wanted to be perceived as a crude, insensitive person who for his seniority's sake would make someone else less important and insulted. Emotions were high; there was no clear protocol in this case, but even if there had been one it would be interpreted as an insult to one or the other.

A quick decision had to be made and the one who blinked first would be damned. I saw two wise and experienced Jordanian politicians in a real-time drama. Many spectators were there at the arena and everyone understood what was at stake. As they approached the door, Zaid Al-Rifaí made a gesture to Al-Majali to proceed first. It was too easy and too complicated all at once. Al-Rifaí is kind but perhaps more senior because of his current position as Speaker, but had Al-Majali exited first, it may have been interpreted as being disrespectful of Al-Rifaí. Al-Majali with a smiling gesture turns to Al-Rifaí and responded "No, you first." Al-Rifaí insisted that Al-Majali proceed first. Mutawí in the middle did not interfere; he left it to the Masters.

Another round was in progress with hands, palms and smiles. One wouldn't want to disappoint his fans and take the back seat, right? Al-Rifaí tried another salvo but with no results or progress on the ground. One can fantasize what would happen if both of them misread or misinterpreted the other simultaneously and proceeded forward a'la Laurel and Hardy or Charlie Chaplin (this actually happened to Israeli Prime Minister Barak with Arafat). The traffic jam at the doorstep worsened during the seconds pass; no one entered and no one left. It was left for the Masters to sort it out without harming each other and time was running out. Someone had to pull out a magic card. And then Al-Rifaí spelled out the magic formula "You are older than me, Abu Samer (Al-Majalí's oldest son is called Samer, and it is a custom in Arab societies that you are nicknamed after your son as "Father of …), you have the priority."

This episode holds in nutshell a lot of life's wisdom, sensitivity, and tact. One can learn a lot from this, if he still thinks that he has something to learn from a neighbor.

CURSING THE EGYPTIANS

When we arrived in Jordan, we realized that people there did not have any clue about Judaism, so we decided to introduce them to some basics through food. My wife, Annette, would cook Jewish food. We would photocopy pages from Ruth Sirkis's* cookbooks and explain to our guests what each dish symbolized. It worked very well and people were very grateful, especially for the culinary knowledge they obtained about Passover foods, including the Matzo and matzo ball soup.

One year we invited some of our Jordanian friends, Muslims and Christians, for a Seder, which is the traditional Passover meal celebrating the Exodus of the Jews from Egypt. Many people do not know that the "Last Supper" was actually a Seder meal. The Passover meal is an interesting one, because it combines a heavy meal with reading the Hagaddah, which is the story and adventures of the Exodus and settling some accounts with the Pharaoh, who enslaved the Jews in Egypt.

As the meal progressed, we were reading chapters of the Hagaddah. Then one of our Christian friends, who was very educated, but also very naughty, started showing signs of impatience. When I asked him what was the matter, he asked me, gleefully, to the amazement of the Muslims, "When do we read the chapter where we curse the Egyptians for what they have done to the Children of Israel?"

It was a nice way for a proud Jordanian to settle national accounts with the Big Sister/Brother-Egypt through the Jews.

*Sirkis, Ruth: A Taste of Tradition; 1972, Ward Ritchie Press, Los Angeles
*Sirkis, Ruth: Popular Food From Israel, 1975, 1985, R. Sirkis Pub. Ltd, Tel Aviv

THE DESCENDANTS OF LAWRENCE'S FRIENDS

Being a collector of books about T. E. Lawrence (Lawrence of Arabia) I found my stay in Jordan quite interesting. Lawrence's activities were closely associated with the Hashemite Family and their revolt against the Turks ("The Arab Revolt" during World War I). Many of his associates, mainly from Al Huweitat and Bani Sakhr tribes, have children and grandchildren who are active today in Jordan. One of T. E. Lawrence's associates was Shakir bin Zeid, who in 1921 became Prince Abdallah's advisor on tribal affairs. His son, Sherif Zeid bin Shakir (1934-2002) was, for many years, Chief of Staff of the Jordanian Army, and, in 1995, he was Prime Minister of Jordan. Shakir bin Zeid, who died in 1936, was regarded by T. E. Lawrence, as a brave and courageous soldier.

In 1995, a book was published about Shakir bin Zeid and printed by the Military Publishing House. I saw a review of the book in one of the newspapers, but it was not available in the bookshops. One day, I accompanied my Ambassador, Professor Shimon Shamir (I also had the privilege to work with him when he served as Israel's Ambassador to Cairo) to a meeting with the Prime Minister Zeid bin Shakir. Around the time the meeting was approaching its end, I asked whether I could ask something. Since I was the one who took the notes in the meeting everyone assumed that I had some technical question for the clarification of my notes. That is a very accepted practice in order to avoid misunderstandings.

I then said that I read about the new book, which was published about the Prime Minister's father and that I was not able to get a copy. Well, I got, on the spot, a copy of the book, with the Prime Minister's dedication. A few months later, the book was available in the open market.

THE DRUZE CONNECTION

The ethnic mosaic of Jordan is kaleidoscopic. From what seems at a first glance as homogenous or perhaps, bi-generic (East Jordanian Bedouins and Palestinians), one discovers, step by step, how heterogeneous Jordan really is, containing much more than meets the eye: from Lebanese Muslims, or Maronites, who escaped Beirut's Civil War to sink into Amman's serenity and tolerance, to Circassians, Chechens, Armenians, Iraqis, and Druze.

We even found Jewish women, who married Palestinians before 1948 only to become refugees with their husbands, and others who married Palestinians in the 70's to move with them to Jordan for one reason or another in the 80's.

While all the other groups keep a visible profile and proudly announce their ethnic origins, the Druze community (who mostly live in Lebanon, Syria or Israel; about 15,000 live in Jordan and a small contingent also in the U.S.A., Canada, and Australia) keeps quite a low profile in Jordan.

One day, I was speeding in a Jordanian car and got stopped by a policeman. Since, for security reasons, we drove cars with regular license plates, he couldn't have known that I was a diplomat. While presenting him my I.D. and license, I noticed that he was holding in his hand a braided plastic lanyard-like key chain with blue, yellow, white, red and green colors. I suspected that he was a Druze because those are the colors of the Druze flag, but I let it go and left the initiative to him. The policeman looked at my diplomatic I.D. and asked where I came from (though it is clearly written on my I.D). I responded that I was from Israel.

He looked at me and asked, "Israeli Jewish or Israeli non-Jewish?"

I pacified him by declaring that I was 100% Jewish.

He then said, "You know that you were speeding?"

I responded that I didn't notice, but I'd take his word for it. That was certainly a very non-Middle Eastern answer, which probably confirmed my Jewishness.

Then came the "Big Bang." He asked me whether I knew Druze in Israel, to which I answered positively, mentioning famous Druze villages on Mt. Carmel: *Daliyat Alkarmel* and *Usafiyyeh.* This did the trick. Upon relaxing, he disclosed that he was a Druze.

A nice chat followed. He mentioned that he had relatives in a mixed village in the Galilee. I asked him whether he visited Israel, and he responded that as a member of the security forces, he'd need a special permit to do that. After a while, it was time for me to be discharged from this encounter.

He let me go, didn't write a ticket, and gave me a useful tip: there was another police trap up the road manned also by a Druze policeman. For practical considerations, I slowed down, so as not to be stopped by him.

NOTE: The Druze in Jordan are known better not as "Druze," but as members of the "Bani Ma'aruf" tribe.

EAST OF EDEN (THE HIJAZI RAILWAY)

One of the important developments at the turn of the Twentieth Century in (Trans) Jordan was the erection of the Hijazi Railway from Damascus to Al-Madinah in the Hijaz (now known as Saudi Arabia). The railway, which was initiated by the Sultan (The Head of the Ottoman Empire) in Istanbul, was both a religious enterprise, designed to ease the access of the Muslims to Mecca for the traditional pilgrimage (*Al-Hajj*), and also a strategic means to ease the transfer of Turkish troops to Far Arabia. The construction, which started in 1900, ended in Al-Madinah in 1908.

The route of the railway passes via Amman and Maan, and during W.W.I. it became the focus of T. E. Lawrence's raids. The Arab troops, which were part of the Arab revolt (Revolt in the Desert), sabotaged the railway, thus attracting many Turkish troops to protect it. They also blew up the telegraph lines along it, compelling the Turks to communicate with Al-Madinah wirelessly and thus provided the British Intelligence with extra Sigint oportunities. Most of the railway passed through Jordan on the edge of the desert or through it.

I was told a nice story about this railway. A Jordanian Parliamentary delegation visited the Netherlands in the 50's. The members were taken for a tour around the country and, of course, were very impressed by the evergreen meadows and the plentifulness of water. One member of the delegation, a Bedouin from the South of Jordan, remarked upon seeing those meadows, that they were probably the Garden of Eden, which is mentioned in the Holy Koran. Another member of the delegation, who was intrigued by the comparison, asked him, "If this is Paradise, where is Hell?"

The Bedouin, without blinking, answered, "East of the Hijazi Railway," referring to the harsh desert conditions.

EDUCATING FOR PEACE

One of the most tragic mistakes of the Arab leaders is their reluctance to educate their people for peace with Israel. Most of the leaders fan the flames of enmity and hatred (of course in different degrees and volumes), but the bottom line is that they promote the demonization of the Israelis (and sometimes the Jews as a whole) and blame them for all the evils and ills of the Middle East and the World.

This, of course, backfires when they make peace with Israel, catching their people unaware and not ready for the surprising turn of events.

The Muslims celebrate each year the month of Ramadan, which is a month of fasting. One is not allowed to eat or drink from dawn to dusk. Then, at a certain moment, a call is heralded from the minarets (and on radio and TV), which marks the beginning of the *Iftar*, or the breaking of the fast.

The first days of the Ramadan *Iftar* are spent with the family. All the brothers and sisters will meet in the home of one of them on a rotary basis, spending time eating and socializing until late after midnight. It is a nice and cheerful event, but after a week or ten days, everyone has had enough of being with the family, and they will start going to *Iftars* outside the family's circle, i.e. with friends and sometimes in restaurants.

Druing the first Ramadan in Amman after the opening of the Israeli Embassy, early in 1995, Einat Schlain-Michael, our Political Second Secretary, and I were invited for an *Iftar* in a restaurant by an East Jordanian businesswoman. Another two couples, both East Jordanians, joined us. The atmosphere was nice and so was the food.

Naturally, we started chatting after filling our bellies. One of the participants needed salt and pepper, which were "parked" near me. I passed them to him. He thanked me graciously and I added in Egyptian dialect, "*Ai khidmah ya fandem,*" which means, "How can I help you? What service can I bestow upon you? Just say it, Sir."

He was surprised by my Egyptian "virtue" (we lived in Cairo between 1987-1989), and I explained that I am a "peace veteran," enjoying peace with Egypt and Jordan. He didn't find it funny. I realized that and asked him what was the matter. Here is almost verbatim what he told me:

"Mr. Yaaqub (Jacob in Arabic), you are our guests tonight; we sit around the same table and you even forward to me, in a friendly manner, the salt and pepper. But it is not easy for us to share a table with you.

"You see, until yesterday, you were the worst enemy. The worst and the dirtiest, and then suddenly, you are a friend and a 'good neighbor.' We are very loyal to His Majesty King Hussein, and if he decided to make peace with Israel, he probably knew what he was doing, and we support his decision.

"But be aware that since 1948, for 47 years, we were educated and brainwashed that you were monsters, vicious and betraying. And now, suddenly, we share with you a table and have to forget all that. Believe me, Mr. Yaaqub and Madam Einat, it is difficult for us."

A few months later, my family joined me in Amman. My wife, Annette, is of Dutch/Slovak origin and speaks English without an accent. She became friendly with Dutch and British ladies who had lived a long time in Amman and looked just like one of them. More than once, she encountered exclamations of disbelief from Jordanians after she responded to their inquiries that she was Jewish, married to an Israeli diplomat.

"*La mush mumkin*" (no, it is impossible). "You are too nice and too decent to be an Israeli or to be Jewish," or, "no, it can't be – you are not aggressive."

ELECTRICAL RELATIONS

This is a story about early Jordanian-Israeli relations, which I heard from Ambassador Moshe Sasson, who was my ambassador in Cairo. He belongs to the first generation of Israeli diplomats and was involved from 1948 with his late father Eliahu (Elias) Sasson in secret negotiations between Golda Meir and King Abdallah I.

Following the war of 1948/9, Jordan was left almost totally without electricity after the destruction of the Rutenberg Electricity Plant in Naharayim (Al-Baqura) in the Upper Jordan Valley. The Israelis who were conducting secret negotiations with King Abdallah hoping to reach a peace agreement with Jordan (which was concluded finally by his grandson King Hussein in 1994) noticed that Jordan was badly affected by the shortage of electricity and at a certain stage offered to connect Jordan to the Israeli electricity grid. This would have supplied Jordan with the electricity it so badly needed.

The wise and experienced King Abdallah listened carefully to the offer and had only one question of clarification: "Who would hold the keys to the shut-off switch?"

The Israelis, who were supposed to be the suppliers, responded automatically, "We, of course."

Upon hearing the answer, the King responded: "It means that I will depend on your moods. No, thank you; I do not need electricity."

A lot has changed since then. The Peace Agreement between Israel and Jordan regulates the annual supply of 50 million cubic meters of water from Israel to Jordan. (See: The Fish is "on the house" on page 61.)

THE END OF THE WORLD (A PALESTINIAN JOKE)

The following is a joke I heard in Amman from both East Jordanians and Palestinians. It may be interpreted in many ways, but certainly indicates the self-image of the Palestinians.

One day, God was fed up with the World and the non-stop troubles He had to deal with. So, He decided to destory the World, i.e., all the Nations, which were the source of his troubles. All the Nations came to heaven, and from there they were assigned to Paradise, such as the Dutch and the Danes, or to Hell, such as the Americans, Russians, Israelis, etc. By the time the Palestinians showed up, both Paradise and Hell were fully occupied and there were no vacancies for the Palestinians. They begged the Angels to let them in, even into Hell, but to no avail. There were no room left.

The Palestinians literally raised Hell to get a solution for their problem. So, the Angels turned to God, explained the situation to Him, and asked Him what to do. God heard their problem and said: "Send them to refugee camps."

FATHERS AND SONS (A TRIBUTE TO IVAN TURGENEV)

Succession in the Middle East is a complicated issue. While one can understand the logic of succession in Kingdoms, the same cannot be said about non-royalty. Grooming one's son as a future Leader/President creates mixed reactions and jokes. Here is one, which I heard in 1998 from a Jordanian, who visited Syria and heard it in Damascus.

The Syrian Intelligence (*Mukhabarat*) decided to plant a "sophisticated" spy in Israel. They recruited a fair-looking Syrian, taught him the Jewish religion, Jewish History, English, and Business Administration. For these tasks, they designated top professors in Syria's universities and trained him for three years.

The plan was to send him via London, posing as a new Jewish immigrant from the U. K., who would settle in Israel and start a business.

Well, after three years of intensive training, they dispatched him with the relevant (but false) documentation to London. There he changed identity and applied for an immigrant visa at the Israeli Embassy. He arrived in Israel and a week later was exposed by the Israeli counter intelligence and brought to trial for spying. Subsequently, he was sentenced to twenty years in prison.

A few years later, so goes the joke, a peace agreement was signed between Syria and Israel, which included, of course, mutual exchange of spies, etc. The Syrian spy was released and, upon arrival at Damascus airport, was immediately detained by his Syrian operators who were puzzled and frustrated by his early exposure, despite the very careful and sophisticated cover.

They asked him what went wrong and he replied that he didn't know. They decided to reconstruct with him his moves, step by step, to try to find out where he had committed his fatal mistake. So they asked whether he destroyed the Syrian documents upon arrival in London and he responded, "Yes."

They asked him whether there was any problem in the Israeli Embassy with getting the visa, and he said, "No." So, they continued the debriefing about his landing in Israel, getting an Israeli I.D. from the Ministry of the Interior, which also went smoothly. They asked what he did next, and he explained, in detail, that he rented an apartment, opened a bank account and rented an office space to start his business, which was also a smooth process.

They asked what he did next and he explained that he furnished the office and hung on the wall photos of Prime Minister Netanyahu and Netanyahu's son (in Syria and elsewhere, the custom is to hang the photographs of the leader and his son, the designated successor, on every available wall).

THE FISH IS "ON THE HOUSE"

One of the most important and intricate agreements between Jordan and Israel is the Water Agreement. Many talented people in both countries were involved in it, and they were all trying to strike the best deal possible for the sakes of their countries. They also had to keep in mind that the limited water resources had to be shared by the Palestinian Authority, with its growing population, Israel, and Jordan. It was the shared attitude of all Israeli Prime Ministers, starting with the late Rabin, followed by Peres, Netenyahu, Barak, and Sharon (who served under Netenyahu as Minister of National Infrastructures in charge of water), that water should be shared with Jordan. It is not healthy to have a thirsty neighbor.

One of the features of the water agreement was pumping a certain amount of water from the Lake of Galilee via a pipeline to King Abdallah Canal, which runs along the Jordan Valley on the Jordanian side, supplying water both for agriculture in the Valley and to Amman for drinking. The construction of the pipeline was completed in May 1997. The Jordanians organized a ceremony in Al-Addasiyyah, where the pipeline joins the King Abdallah Canal.

The new Israeli Ambassador, Dr. Oded Eran, had not yet presented his credentials, so he couldn't perform officially. I was the *chargé d'affaires* and was invited together with the American, Russian, British, French, Japanese, and German Ambassadors to attend the inauguration of the pipeline by King Hussein. It was a warm day; the time was noon. We sat in a special tent, which was erected for the occasion. The King arrived and before starting the ceremony, he went to see the flow of the water from the pipe to the Canal. It was a steady flow, modest in volume, so we could see small fish, which left the Lake of Galilee via the pipe, to be incorporated in King Abdallah's Canal (named after the first King of Jordan, King Hussein's grandfather).

I accompanied His Majesty and saw him quite amused by the sight of fish, which certainly were not part of the Agreement. His Majesty asked me what fish it was. I grew up in Tiberias, which is on the shore of the Lake of Galilee, and so I had some idea about the different kinds of fish, even if they were small. What we saw was a fish called Musht (which means *comb* in Arabic or *St. Peter's fish* in English) and which is considered a delicacy. The King became even more amused.

Seeing that, I told him, "*Ya Jalalat Almalik – Alsamak Aleina* (Your Majesty, the fish is "on the house").

FROM JERUSALEM TO BEIRUT - A BAGEL SAGA (A TRIBUTE TO THOMAS FRIEDMAN)

Many Arabs, Jordanians, Palestinians, Lebanese, Saudis and Egyptians have studied and lived in the U.S.A. Among the other wonderful American features they were exposed to were Bagels, a traditional Jewish round, boiled and then baked bread, which became part of the American food culture but didn't degenerate to the rank of junk food.

When we arrived in Amman, we, of course, started "importing" from Jerusalem the long awaited bagels from Bonkers Bagels. Unfortunately, they closed down in 2000, leaving us with plenty of coupons for "one dozen free for six dozen bought."

The many different varieties of bagels became an immediate hit. "Normalizing" or "not normalizing" became irrelevant. Just deliver the bagels! Every time we were in Jerusalem we bought a few dozen bagels (with cream cheese of course). And upon return to Amman we quickly distributed them, with the cream cheese (smoked salmon is available in Amman) among friends and foes alike. The poppy seed and the garlic ones were at the top of the list of favorites. One of our friends of Lebanese origin, who like many others studied in the U.S.A., was addicted to bagels. So were his relatives in Beirut.

One day, my wife Annette got an urgent telephone call. Our Lebanese friend had to go very soon to Beirut because an uncle had to undergo surgery. Annette wished the uncle good health and expressed the hope that the surgery would be crowned with success. Then came the real reason for the call: "I want to surprise my relatives with bagels. Do you have some frozen ones?" We were flat out after distributing the last ones a few days earlier.

"When do you leave for Beirut?" asked Annette. He replied that he was leaving tomorrow. I received an urgent call at the Embassy from my wife. "It is urgent," my secretary repeated Annette's words. Annette asked me to "fix it." I checked to see who was in Israel at the moment and who would be returning to Amman that same evening. Luckily, my friend, Consul David Radnitz, was in Jerusalem with a cellular phone. I called him, explained the political importance of the endeavor, and sent him to Bonkers Bagels. Simultaneously, I called the bagel makers to place the order for six dozen (plus a dozen free of charge). David came back at 11:30 PM. By midnight, the bagels were delivered to our Lebanese friend.

The next evening in Beirut, a group of Lebanese graduates of American universities were enjoying the taste of peace.

THE GIRL WITH THE BIGGEST SUITCASE

When we lived in Amman, we met many young educated Palestinians who were born and educated in Kuwait, studied in American or European universities, and were expelled together with their families from Kuwait after the Gulf War in 1991. The Kuwaitis regarded the Palestinians as collaborators with Saddam Hussein and could not forgive Arafat for siding with Iraq, and so with their liberation, the Kuwaitis expelled all the Palestinians.

We found their stories fascinating. Some of them were refugees for the third time in just 43 years: starting in 1948-49, when they moved from their cities and villages to refugee camps in the West Bank. Then for a second time in 1967, when they escaped from the West Bank to Jordan. Many of them left Jordan for Kuwait in the early 70's and then were refugees for the third time when they were expelled in 1991.

Since the Iraqi invasion took place during the summer, when the temperatures reach F120-30 degrees, many of the

Palestinians had left Kuwait for vacation a few weeks earlier to go to Jordan or Europe. Many of them went on vacation with their children (it was a summer school vacation), and, of course, could not return to Kuwait to their homes and property. The psychological impact of the uprooting and inability to go back, especially on the children, was enormous.

We became friendly with a young woman who was forteen years old in 1991. She was abroad during the Iraqi invasion and never went back to Kuwait again. She was very taken by our attitude towards her and our sympathy with the Palestinians, who once again suffered because of mistakes committed by their un-elected leaders. She even convinced her parents to come to a dinner at our house.

She was always in tears while talking about the books and personal affects she left in Kuwait. The trauma of being separated from her favorite affects was so profound that she decided not to leave anything behind while traveling.

"Whenever I travel," she told me, "I take everything dear to me with me: my books, my clothes, and my bears. You see, I can never be sure that I'll be able to go back, so I travel with everything. If you see a girl in the airport with the biggest suitcase, it is me!"

I'M AN INTELLECTUAL. I'M NOT SUPPOSED TO TALK TO YOU.

The attitude of the Arab intellectuals towards Israel or "normalization" with it is mind-boggling. I devoted a lot of thinking and analyzing to it and may have even found a complex explanation (in 1996 in a lecture at Tel-Aviv University, I tried to explain, but I had "lost" my academic audience).

Even before arriving in Amman (in the mid-80's, early 90's), I knew of several Jordanians who would, in broad terms, meet the definition of an intellectual. When I did arrive in 1994 it was possible for me to potentially meet these intellectuals. However, having experience from living in Cairo, I decided to be smart and not to surprise or embarrass anyone, including myself.

There were two people whom I particularly wished to see, and I had to devise a way to do that (one of them knew about me already in 1992). I asked our Jordanian secretary to call this person and tell him that "Jacob Rosen, the new Israeli *chargé d'affaires*, was in town and wished to meet with him but was not sure whether the timing was appropriate."

The answer my secretary got from him was that he understood from the media reports that Jacob Rosen, who opened the Israeli Embassy, was the same person he had heard about from our mutual friend and "*Insha'allah* (with God's will), we would find a suitable time to meet."

In other words, he said a temporary "no" but didn't exclude the possibility at a later time.

At the beginning of 1995, I was invited by the German Ambassador to a reception honoring the Speaker of the German Parliament, who was touring the Middle East. As the guests started dispersing, I stayed a little longer because it was an opportunity for me to meet as many people as possible. Suddenly, a gentleman approached me and asked me, smilingly, whether I knew who he was. I responded that I was new in town but certainly would like to know who he was. He proudly introduced himself as the man who replied to my secretary that he would meet me at a suitable time. We chatted for about half an hour, far after the last of the guests left. The German Ambassador was smiling gleefully at us, making his own contribution to Israeli-Jordanian relations.

The other person I wanted to meet was harder to reach, but I found a prominent Palestinian in Amman, who knew him and convinced him to come to his office and to meet me there "by chance." He agreed. We spoke at length, but I realized that he was not yet ready for a steady relationship.

One day, I met him again at a reception at the Chinese Embassy. I saw him and his wife and chatted with both of them. This time, I had the "*chutzpah*" to suggest that he would be welcome to come to dinner at our home. He looked around and with a bastardly, Middle Eastern smile, replied, "Mr. Rosen, I am an intellectual. I'm not supposed to talk to you."

Well, we have had the honor and pleasure to host these Jordanians at our home more than once. We learned a lot from them and were encouraged by their personal defiance of the rules.

"I HAVE A BELGIAN WIFE"

The Palestinian component in the Jordanian population is quite significant. There are different estimates about the percentage of the Palestinian proportion, some even claiming that the Palestinians constitute more than half of the population in Jordan. Things are more complex than they seem at first glance, since defining who is a Palestinian in Jordan is as complex as defining "Who is a Jew?" on the other side of the Jordan River. "Who is a Palestinian?" is a very subjective state of mind if we take into consideration that the Palestinians arrived in Jordan through several waves of immigration.

There is no clear date for onset or conclusion. Just to illustrate and add to the confusion, one can mention that one of the most influential families in Al-Karak in the south of Jordan (the Al-Majali tribe) arrived there about four centuries ago from Hebron. Some of the prominent families in Al-Salt arrived there by the end of the 19th or the beginning of the 20th century. A family like Touqan arrived from Nablus in 1901 or Al-Bustami in 1884, also from Nablus. The third wife of King Hussein, the late 'Alia' Touqan, was a descendant of this branch. Was she a Palestinian or was she a Jordanian? Who has the right to decide?

Then there are the Palestinians and Syrians who arrived in Amman in the Twenties and established themselves in Jordan. Are they Jordanians or should they be considered, even today, as Syrians or Palestinians? To complicate the matter even further, we should remember that there are cross-marriages between East Jordanians and Palestinians. In most of the cases, it is an East Jordanian male marrying a Palestinian female. This is not a widespread phenomenon, but it occurs in Amman, Irbid, Aqaba and Al-Salt, both among Muslims and Christians. In my estimation, at least 10% of present-day marriages are of this nature. How should we define their children? How do they define themselves?

Our Cultural Attaché (his rank was Minister–Counselor), Victor Nahmias, a native of Cairo, and his wife Ilana, who spoke very little Arabic, were very active socially in Amman. Ilana's English was good and so was her French, as they had lived for a while in Paris. Victor knew Arabic from home. One day, Victor and Ilana spoke to a manager of a hotel in Amman, which resulted in his extending Ilana and Victor an invitation to visit him at his home. To prevent any surprises, under the mistaken assumption that we, the Israelis, may be sensitive to Palestinians, he told Victor, in Arabic "*Zawjati Beljikiyyah*," which literally means, "My wife is Belgian." Ilana, who still encountered difficulties speaking Arabic, responded with joy "Good, so we can talk French."

What Ilana didn't know was that in Jordanian slang, *Belgian* means *Palestinian.* It is not clear what the exact origin of that slang is, but the common version is that during the civil war in 1970 (Black September) the code name for Palestinians by the Jordanian security forces was "Belgian," or "*Beljiki*" in Arabic. It is interesting that a term, which had a very negative connotation in 1970, became a popular and non-offensive term in the Nineties. So what do you do when you want to make a reference to a true Belgian? You just repeat "*Beljiki Beljiki*" (Belgian Belgian), as in "Bond, James Bond."

"INSHALLAH" (WITH GOD'S WILL)

"*Inshallah*" is a word frequently used in the Arab culture, both by Christians and Muslims. It is less a reflection of a deep religious belief and more a state of mind that there is little we can do actively about something, and even if we do so, many things may happen to change it in any case. It's semantic field ranges from a real hope to helplessness, from good will to an excuse and "no." The real challenge of a foreigner is to pick up the right meaning in the right context and, of course, in real time. There are a few similarities in Western-American-Jewish culture such as "I see your point," which basically means "I disagree with you;" or in the American-Jewish slang/joke, "Believe me" sometimes means "go to hell;" or the British way of saying, "We must meet for a drink sometime," or the American's way of saying, "Talk to you later."

The Arabs are polite people and will make every effort not to disappoint you or to say the word "no." Of course, this politeness does not apply to political negotiations, especially Arab-Israeli ones, where the "no" word changes hands frequently. The following story will illustrate the different perceptions/interpretations of *Inshallah*, depending, of course, on your own agenda and understanding.

One day, we had two Israeli Ministers visiting Amman. My Ambassador, Professor Shimon Shamir accompanied one and asked me to accompany the other to a meeting with his Jordanian counterpart. On the way, I tried to brief the Israeli Minister about his counterpart, and the Minister consulted with me about some points he wanted to raise with the Jordanians.

He told me that he intended to invite the Jordanian Minister to visit Israel. I responded that it was a nice idea, but with all due respect I cautioned that, unlike in Israel where the system is different, a Jordanian Minister couldn't accept an invitation unless he had an earlier O.K. from the Prime Minister or the Royal Palace to do so. I added that I did not think he would be able to come, so it would be better not to extend the invitation. The Minister replied in confidence, "I know the Arabs; he'll come."

We entered the office of the Jordanian Minister. They chatted about their Ministries and at a certain point, the Israeli thanked the Jordanian Minister for receiving him and invited him to visit on the reciprocal basis. The Jordanian Minister thanked him for the invitation and in a nonchalant manner, he added "*Inshallah*."

Our Minister didn't get the point and asked, "So, when can you come?" The Jordanian responded that at the moment the Parliament was discussing the budget, and he had to be in town. Our Minister continued to press, "When is the budget debate over?"

The Jordanian Minister said, "It will take a while. You know how budget debates are." The Israeli Minister continued, "So, come after the Parliament session is over." The Jordanian started sweating under his collar and responded in a hidden impatience, after realizing that our Minister didn't get the point, "*Inshallah*, I'll visit."

The meeting was over and we returned to the car. The Israeli Minister turned to me and with a victorious smile, told me, "You see, Jacob, he accepted my invitation despite your skepticism. I told you I know them!

Needless to say, we are still waiting for him to visit Israel.

I WANT MY PROPERTY BACK

After the opening of the Israeli Embassy in Amman in 1994, we started receiving calls from Jordanians, both of Palestinian and East Bank origin, who were inquiring about the possibility of getting back the property which they owned in Mandatory Palestine until 1948, and which is now in Israel. They came to our office and presented the original documents, confirming their ownership, be it land or real estate.

Some of those who came were old people and some were their children. Some of them seemed well to do and others, quite poor. But it was important to them, as a matter of principle, to confirm their rights to that property.

Of course, we entered into long dialogues and monologues about wrong and right, justice and injustice.

Many of them were surprised when I told than that in the neighboring rooms were my colleagues whose families hailed from Egypt and Iraq, who were in possession of similar documents about property left by Jews in Arab countries.

I tried to explain to them that their request was part of a much larger problem and that one day, when we have peace with all the Arab States, where Jews lived formerly, there would be a chance to deal with their claims and the Jewish/Israeli counter claims. I indicated that the Government of Israel and WOJAC (World Organization of Jews from Arab Countries) were registering the property Jews left in Arab countries and one day the claims of both sides should be settled by some mechanism.

Needless to say, most of my visitors were surprised to learn about Jewish property left in Arab countries. Some tried to find out how this mechanism would work. I replied that I did not know, but I could only assume that the Government of Israel would represent the Jewish claimants who settled in Israel, and probably the Arab States would do the same.

The almost unanimous response to that was sheer disappointment. "Mr. Rosen," they said, "your government is a democratic one, and we are sure that it will pay your private citizens whatever they deserve. If the Arab governments represent us, we will never see a penny."

THE JEWS OF 1967

Terminology in the Middle East is not just terminology. It is a state of mind, a mirror image of one's own attitudes and beliefs. Terms are coined in different ways and in many cases just by circumstances.

Thus, Palestinians in Jordan who live in refugee camps are called "refugees." If they settled outside the camps, they would be called "citizens" or "Palestinian brothers."

The Arabs who stayed in Israel after the 1948 War are called the "1948 Arabs." This designation distinguishes them from the Arabs in the West Bank and Gaza Strip and avoids the need to mention the traumatic word "Israel."

One evening, I was driving back to Amman from Israel. For security reasons, we always drove rented cars, changing them from time to time to avoid driving permanent vehicles with diplomatic plates.

For some reason there was a temporary roadblock set up by the Jordanian police not far away from the border crossing.

A police officer indicated to me to stop the car, and in a very customary and polite manner, he said in Arabic, "Good evening."

In Jordan, other than a matter of courtesy, this is also a practical way of "profiling by accent." In most of the cases, the accent will disclose your identity or the geographical area you come from.

I responded as well, "Good evening," but somehow, and not surprisingly, the officer could not identify my origin.

"Are you coming from the West Bank?" he tried again. I answered that I was driving back from Jerusalem.

This gave him an additional hint that I may be somehow connected to Israel, but probably was not Jewish. My Arabic was effectual and sounded, somehow, like urban Jordanian.

"Are you a tourist?" he tried further.

"No," I replied in confidence.

"Are you from the '1948 Arabs'?" ('*Arab Tamania Warba'in*')?" he tried again.

His suspicions about my being an Israeli Arab had good foundation. Many Israeli Arabs, especially those from mixed cities and with an academic education, have adopted a slightly Hebrew/Yuppie accent, and the accent sounds unfamiliar to East Jordanian Bedouins.

At that stage, I thought it would be unfair to continue this "cat and mouse" game with a decent law enforcement officer and responded, "No, I'm from the Jews of 1967" (1967 is a very traumatic date in modern Arab history because of the defeat of Arab armies in the "Six Day War" that year).

I pronounced it clearly, so that he could hear it well. Of course he had never heard such a term before, and it took him a few seconds to grasp what it meant. When it finally percolated, he smiled and said, "*Allah Ma'ak*" (May God be with you) and indicated that I could proceed. I finally told him who I was. He started laughing, his white teeth shining in the Jordan Valley darkness.

THE KING OFFERS CONDOLENCES IN ISRAEL

In March, 1997, a Jordanian soldier on guard in Albaqura, in the northern part of the Jordan Valley, opened fire on a group of Israeli school girls who were visiting the area, killing seven of them and wounding more. It was a shock to all of us and a reminder of how fragile the peace is and how harmful uncontrolled hatred and ignorance can be.

King Hussein, who was at the time of the fatal shooting on a visit to Spain, immediately cut short his visit and returned to Jordan. There he offered a public apology to the Israeli people, and, in an unprecedented gesture of humanity, he decided to come to Israel and offer his condolences to each of the bereaved families during the seven days of mourning, as practiced in the Jewish tradition (*Shiv'ah*, which means seven in Hebrew).

According to Jewish religious customs (the girls were from religious backgrounds), while mourning the dead, the mourners sit on the floor. The visitors refrain from saying words of greeting upon entering or leaving the house and occasional prayers are recited. It is also the custom that the door stays open or unlocked and no one greets or receives at the door. Visitors who come to mourn offer their sympathies.

Needless to say, the Arabs' (both Muslim and Christian, as well as the Druze) mourning customs do differ from the Jewish ones. First of all, the mourning period is only three days. There is segregation/separation between males and females. The protocol is totally different. In the Arab mourning tradition, male relatives of the deceased stand in a row outside the gate or door to honor, receive, and greet the visitors.

Upon entering the house, the guests are offered a seat on a chair or couch or "fauteille," according to their social status and will be served a cup of bitter Arabic coffee. One should spend 15-20 minutes, and, by the time he is offered another cup of coffee, it is about time to leave.

Now imagine this.... His Majesty, the King of Jordan, who rarely pays personal condolences visits in Jordan, takes the exceptional step of visiting seven families in Israel to offer condolences for the murder of their daughters by one of his soldiers. The Jordanians, who are stunned by the whole event, are further amazed to see that their King is not even received by anyone at the doorstep (except for security personnel) and is not even offered a seat but rather has been seated unroyally on the floor.

Later, more than once, I heard the comment: "How could you humiliate our King? Why would you sit him on the floor?"

No doubt we have an enormous educational challenge here.

Kosher Breakfast in Amman, Kosher Dinner in Amman (When the King Asks You Don't Refuse)

The influx of Israeli tourists to Jordan after the establishment of relations between the two countries, along with the opening of the Embassies in Tel Aviv and Amman, created a new set of problems and challenges—some of them culinary. Some Israeli Jews adhere to *kashrut* (kosher) regulations (religious dietary laws), with some of them observing the regulations more strictly than others.

Many Israelis felt that they must see Petra, an ancient city engraved in stone, which was a legend in Israel. Some wanted to visit Mount Nebo, from where Moses saw the Promised Land. Some wanted to visit Aaron's Tomb and some just wanted a general tour.

The question, for *kashrut* keeping Jews, was how to keep the dietary laws in Jordan (the members of the Embassy had a special arrangement with a supermarket in Jerusalem). At a certain point, Israeli and Jordanian entrepreneurs opened a kosher restaurant in Amman, but it proved to be very complicated. Since the Jordanians would not allow the import of meat from Israel under a variety of pretexts and having a *schochet* (ritual slaughterer) in Amman was also impractical, the restaurant closed after only a few weeks.

One day, we were informed that the whole National Religious Party (N.R.P.) faction in the Knesset (Israel's Parliament) would be visiting Jordan for a few days. I was asked to come to their hotel to brief them over breakfast. I came to the dining room wondering how they would manage with food.

Well, the Israeli travel agency, which made the arrangements for them, found out that many hotels in Amman employed Palestinians who had worked previously in hotels in Israel and were fully acquainted with *kashrut* regulations. Many of them worked in the Hilton or Sheraton hotels in Tel Aviv or Jerusalem, spoke Hebrew, and could perform according to *kashrut*'s rules and regulations.

The group brought fresh rolls and cheese from Israel and deposited them in the hotel's kitchen. The rest was left to the kosher-trained Palestinian staff. The staff served the rolls, cheese, olives, and vegetables, to the satisfaction of the Israeli parliamentarians and their spouses. I went to talk to the kitchen staff and they proudly declared in Hebrew that they could perform the job, even without the presence of the *mashgiach* (a *kashrut* supervisor, who is present in every kitchen in Israeli hotels).

But this was an easy situation compared to one that took place in February 1995. Mr. Eitan Haber, the energetic and resourceful Chief of the Office of the late Yitzhak Rabin, initiated and organized an invitation for dinner in the Royal Palace with His Majesty King Hussein for the leaders of factions and committees in the Israeli Knesset, all in all, about 32 Members — Arab and Jew, strict Orthodox and total sinners. This created a delicate situation because when you accept an invitation from a King (in Judaism, you even have a special blessing to say while meeting a King), you do not refuse to eat what he is offering.

On the other hand, some MK's are very orthodox and, of course, could not touch the food. Here was a situation perfect for the classic role of diplomacy: tact, common sense and goodwill. I got an urgent call one morning from Eitan Haber, informing me in a clandestine manner about the dinner which was to be offered that same evening. He urged me to go quickly to the Royal Palace to supervise the seating arrangements (since their Jordanian parliamentary counterparts would be there as well), and make special arrangements for the MK's who observe *kashrut* laws. I obeyed the orders and went to the Palace where Col. Ali Shukri, the Chief of the Office of His Majesty, met me.

I looked at the seating arrangements and the name cards of each guest and asked the Chef to accompany me. Whenever I saw a name of an ultra-orthodox guest, I drew two stars on the card. That meant plastic plates and utensils plus lettuce and washed, but uncut, fruits and vegetables. In other cases, when I was in doubt, I drew only one star, which meant no fish or meat, just vegetarian.

I think I performed well; no complaints were heard from the respective guests about the "food arrangements."

KUWAITI TRAFFIC LAWS

One-way to estimate the attitudes of people, vis-à-vis other people, is to hear their jokes. If you are careful, or lucky, you might even reveal the intricate wirings of nerve and mind, which culminate in what is called mood (please read this sentence again to absorb it's full meaning).

One hears a lot of stories about the Palestinians in Kuwait — about how they perceived that their Kuwaiti hosts treated them. I presume that there is another side to the story and that one should also listen to the Kuwaiti version, which I hope to have an opportunity to do some day.

Here is one Palestinian joke which, I think, tells it all, from one angle at least:

"A car is approaching a roundabout.

Another car is already circling in the roundabout.
Which car has the priority?

The Kuwaiti, of course."

MIDDLE EASTERN ESTIMATES

One of the real challenges in the Middle East is to get reliable economic data. This data is crucial for investors and businessmen who consider ventures in the region and need it for decision making.

Many businessmen who have tried in vain to get the data ended at our doorstep, asking for help and verification of the numbers given to them by potential Arab partners. Our attempts to call different institutions to verify or to find data sometimes yielded answers such as: "We do not know too much about that company; however, our records indicate that they didn't pay membership fees in recent years."

Stopping a Bedouin on the highway from Amman to Aqaba to inquire about the closest gas station may yield an answer such as: "Two cigarettes," which means the time it takes to smoke two cigarettes. Once we heard an answer, "*kil-killein*," which means one or two kilomteres (it was actually seven).

This reminds me of an Egyptian anecdote. Until the early 80's, there were almost no apples grown in Egypt, due to climatic factors. However, about that time, some Egyptians managed to get "Ana" apple trees from Sinai. The Israelis introduced "Ana" to the Sinai (when they were in control of it after the 1967 war), since it adapted itself well to arid/desert climate and soil.

Some Egyptian entrepreneurs realized the potential and believed that other apple varieties could also be grown in Egypt with the proper expertise and technology. This was, by the way, one of our contributions to the development and proliferation of agricultural production in Egypt.

One day in 1988, an Israeli expert on apple orchards visited Egypt to advise to this affect. He visited a farm of an Egyptian who was of Palestinian origin, and who had the biggest apple orchard in Egypt at that time. He was quite impressed by what he saw and asked his host how many feddans (hectares) of apple orchards existed in Egypt. The host thought for a moment and answered that "about 600 hectares." The Israeli, slightly surprised, asked, "That's all?" Feeling that the guest was disappointed, the host thought for a minute and then answered: "Do you know what? Maybe 2,000."

I have another story about the population in Cairo, which deserves a separate chapter.

MY FOREFATHERS WERE RIGHT, WEREN'T THEY?

Opening the borders between Israel and Jordan in 1994 provided the Israeli Arab citizens with the opportunity to meet for the first time relatives who left their cities and villages following the 1948 Arab-Israeli war. For the younger generation it was an opportunity to meet their relatives who were born in Jordan after 1948. It was a very interesting and soul searching encounter since many of those who were in Jordan lived in refugee camps while their Israeli relatives were in much better shape, in many respects. Some of the Israeli Arabs whom I know brought their newly discovered relatives to visit me in the Embassy for a variety of reasons: either to prove to their refugee relatives (who considered those who stayed in Israel as Quislings and collaborators with the Zionists) that their status was sound and that they had good relations with their authorities or to arrange the initial contact for granting their relatives a visa to visit them in Israel.

It was a fascinating lesson for me to follow the dynamics of such courtesy visits to my office. It took some time before I figured out what was going on. I realized that it was more important for the Israeli Arabs to meet me and "show off" rather than the visa technicalities which their relatives were interested in. The longer the hugs with me lasted (men hug each other when they meet in Jordan), the longer the soul searching nights would be that they spent with relatives in Jordan.

From what I managed to reconstruct, I gather that those family encounters were intensely and bitterly dedicated to comparing notes about what happened to those who stayed in Israel in 1948 and those who decided to leave for variety of reasons. In the mid 90's the economic situation of many Israeli Arabs was relatively sound while many of those in Jordan still lived as refugees.

One day I was visited by an Israeli Arab friend of mine. We spoke at length about a range of issues. By the time he stepped out of my office I wondered loudly why he didn't ask me to arrange a visa for his newly discovered cousin in Irbid (north Jordan). He responded seriously and painfully that his cousin would not visit him in Israel. I naturally wondered and asked "Why?" The answer was, "My cousin told me that if he would visit me in Israel it would be an admission that his grandfather's decision to leave in 1948 was wrong."

THE 1948 - GENERATION

I was born in 1948 in Poland, to parents who miraculously survived the Holocaust. Because of this virtue of nature, I didn't participate in the war of 1948 and was not part of its victories or defeats. This is not an empty statement. It allowed me, during our stay in Amman, to talk to Palestinians of my age group in a slightly detached way.

I met many people who hailed from Mandatory Palestine and who had lived in Jordan since 1948. Talking to the older generation was not easy, since most of them saw Israel as the cardinal reason for their living in Jordan and not West of the Jordan River. However, it was easier to talk to their children and grandchildren who, like me, didn't take part in the 1948 war.

The standard version, which I heard repeatedly, was: "We were expelled." I became intrigued, because I know very well that following the 1948 war, not all the Arabs left Israel and significant concentrations of them stayed in the Negev Desert, the Triangle and the Galilee. They stayed not only in villages, but also in cities such as Jaffa, Ramleh, Lod, Haifa, Acre, and, of course, Nazareth.

Occasionally, and in proper circumstances, I would ask some of my Palestinian peers to explain to me how or why their parents/grandparents left in 1948. I would add that since neither they nor I participated in the 1948 war, it would be easier for us to talk about it.

The range of honest answers surprised me: stories about surrender and expulsion, panic, confusion, escaping, following the leadership, tactical/temporary departure to protect the family from the raging battles, shock at seeing the Arab armies withdrawing from the places they were supposed to protect, etc.

All of those were more or less the stories or accounts one expected to hear. But there was an extra version, or account, which was new to me and which I heard several times from Palestinians, especially those from upper classes and urban backgrounds who had business and professional contacts with Jews in Mandatory Palestine. It seemed that there were cases in which Jews offered protection and assurance to their Arab neighbors/partners. The Jews assured them that if they stayed and did not participate in the hostilities, they would be able to guarantee that they and their families would stay intact.

Naturally, I asked what happened and why they didn't stay. Well, here comes the painful part. They couldn't afford to stay because this would have been considered an act of treason and an indication of cooperation with the enemy. In other words, some Palestinians were guaranteed protection by their Jewish neighbors, but they were afraid that their stay under Jewish patronage would be viewed as treason. So, they left as well.

NO, SHE IS KUWAITI

Among the most interesting groups that we encountered in Jordan were the Palestinians who were expelled from Kuwait following the Gulf War in 1991. The "Palestinian Experience in Kuwait" as it was coined, began in the early 50's and reached its zenith in the 80's. About 400,000 Palestinians lived in Kuwait.

They held positions in the free professions, in teaching, and, of course, in business. They were the middle class and the backbone of economic and academic life, prolific in journalism and literarture. Some of them lived there for more than thirty years, had their children born and educated there in the top Arab and foreign schools (The New English School, The American School of Kuwait, The International School of Kuwait, etc.).

Upon graduation, many of those young people, who were fluent in English, were admitted to American universities either in Cairo, Beirut, or the USA and/or Canada. The education and first language of their professional expression was English. Their business cards were "Yuppyish."

They are very talented, young, ambitious and open minded. After 1994, many of them visited the Palestinian Authority and were quite depressed by the fact that the PA was not interested in their talents or education.

The life stories of the Palestinians with Kuwaiti background are fascinating, and I could fill volumes with them (there is almost no literature, as of yet, about this group). Most of them came back to Jordan in 1991 with professional experience and some with money as well. Some of them were eligible for compensation for the property they left in Kuwait and were looked upon with envy by both the East Jordanians and the Palestinians who stayed in Jordan (many of them in refugee camps).

It is a very interesting sociological and anthropological phenomenon. One of the best representatives of this group is Queen Rania, the wife of King Abdullah II. She was born in Kuwait in 1971 to Palestinian parents (her father, a medical doctor), and she was educated in the New English School and studied Business Administration at American University in Cairo.

One day, an American researcher came to Amman and interviewed a respected Palestinian about the status and prospects of the Palestinians in Jordan. The man complained that the Palestinians were discriminated against by the authorities and were not getting their fair share. The visitor, who was quite surprised, said, "What are you talking about? The Queen is Palestinian!"

The response he got was: "No, she is not Palestinian. She is Kuwaiti." When he asked for clarification, the Palestinian added that the Palestinians who came back from

Kuwait were a separate group. They lived in their own closed circle, spoke their own slang, and frequented the same Palestinian doctors, dentists, and accountants they had in Kuwait. In short they were not integrating with the rest of the Palestinians who lived in Jordan.

THE NORMALIZING PET

One of the most amazing and disturbing phenomena of the Peace between the Arab States and Israel is the unrelenting opposition which it faces from the Arab intellectuals and professional associations, who are vigorously against any contact with Israel or what they term as "normalizing with the enemy" (*Tatbi'*). One would have assumed that it would be the illiterate masses who would be against normalization, while the intellectuals would be in the avant-garde of those who want to break the walls of hatred. But, in fact, the opposite is true.

All the professional organizations, which include doctors, lawyers, engineers, journalists, veterinarians, dentists, etc., in Jordan and Egypt adopted a policy of actually boycotting Israel and punishing any of their members who maintained contact with the Israelis. It is quite complicated because, in many cases, the punishment is the withdrawal of membership of the "violator, normalizer." The problem is that one cannot, by law, practice his profession without being a member of that professional association. This in turn creates comic and tragic situations, such as when a Minister in the Cabinet, who was also a member of one of these associations, visited Israel or received his Israeli counterpart.

This does not mean that we did not have medical treatment in Amman, but many times, we faced "edgy" situations.

We had a dog in Amman, which we brought with us from Israel. He was a cross between a Labrador Retriever and a German Shepherd. We had a local vet who was interested in neither the dog's nor in his owners' nationality. But as good and neurotic Jews, we occasionally took our dog to Israel for a second opinion. We were actually the second Israeli family who had a "border-crossing dog," but unlike the other family, we kept a much higher profile and presence in the diplomatic and local community.

And so it was that pet owners in Amman, who encountered some serious problems and needed a second opinion or a complicated surgical procedure, turned to us for advice and guidance. We were glad to explain to them the Israeli veterinary requirements for crossing the border, and sometimes we even coordinated their crossing with the representatives of the Israeli Ministry of Agriculture at the border. After a while, Jordanians started approaching us, asking for help with their pets. They would ask us to fix an appointment for them in Jerusalem or Tel-Aviv. We became "experts" and met some Jordanian pet owners whom we otherwise would probably not have met.

One day my wife Annette happened upon a nice dog that was limping in a yard. She made some inquiries and found out that he was wounded and had been treated, but to no avail. He looked miserable, and his owner was out of town. Annette got very frustrated and left the owner a note on his gate offering help. He called three days later. Annette reprimanded him for his "criminal negligence" and offered to help by taking the dog to Israel. The man almost fainted when he heard the destination. To make a long story short, he was convinced that this was the only solution. I arranged a visa for him, and Annette took them to Israel (the dog had a dislocated hip). Afterwards, we became friends.

After we left Jordan, the situation there deteriorated because of the outbreak of violence in the Palestinian Authority in October 2000, which affected Jordan as well. The "anti-normalization movement," which was established by the professional associations, accelerated its activities, threatening to publicize all the names of the normalizers.

One day we called (from the USA) a mutual friend in Amman, on the occasion of his birthday, and asked him the whereabouts of our dog-owner friend. He replied that our mutual friend was scared of the threat of publishing the names of the normalizers and quoted him as remarking sarcastically: "Oh my Gosh, now they will accuse my dog of normalizing with the enemy."

OUR BEST FIGHTERS ARE TREATED BY THE ENEMY

Combat pilots are universally cherished by every nation, as their crème de la crème—the best, the bravest, etc. Socially, they are regarded as a privileged class, with all that such a designation implies.

Jordan is no different in this respect and takes good care of its pilots and other members of its armed forces. In some cases, there is a tendency to send them abroad, mainly to the U.K. and the U.S.A. for medical treatment, which the doctors believe could not be provided at home.

Needless to say, such a practice is very expensive, since it includes the medical costs, airfares, and lodgings for the accompanying relatives. After the establishment of diplomatic relations between Jordan and Israel, it was realized by many (including doctors in the U.S.A.) that in some cases it might be cheaper and more practical to send those military personnel to be treated in Israeli hospitals, especially in spinal-related cases and in orthopedics, in which Israel had, unfortunately, accumulated expertise. And the Jordanians started coming.

In 1997, a special trauma treatment center was inaugurated at Ichilov Hospital in Tel Aviv, in memory of the late Israeli Prime Minister Yitzhak Rabin (his death was actually confirmed in that hospital). Among the many guests who arrived at the ceremony was King Hussein of Jordan, who regarded Yitzhak Rabin as a friend.

The King, who knew many of his military officers personally, asked to visit some of those who were being treated there at that time. As is the custom on such occasions, the Jordanian State TV provided full coverage of His Majesty's movements and his visit to the Jordanian officers in the Israeli hospital.

There was a Jordanian officer who stepped on a land mine, while serving with the UN Peacekeeping Forces in Bosnia, and a helicopter pilot, who suffered spinal injuries after his chopper had crashed.

Many weeks after the visit, I still heard the tremors and aftershocks of the Jordanians' amazement and disbelief that "our best boys" (those who were trained to fight the "Zionist Enemy"), were actually being treated and mended by that very enemy.

New realities percolate slowly!

PARANOIA

Many ways are devised to discourage people from using/consuming products or services. The Middle East/Arab-Israeli conflict is no exception. The case of *Pokemon* in Saudi Arabia is the best known because Islamic edict claimed that the Japanese *Pokemon* cards contained Zionist symbols and as such couldn't be purchased by Muslim believers.

Fundamentalists, whatever their ideology is, are afraid of the Internet because it provides access to free information. Occasionally, they themselves use it to disseminate their own message, ignoring their own aversions.

When I lived in Amman, I heard that among many other arguments Muslim fundamentalist students used to keep away fellow students from the Internet, was a claim that the search engine, "Yahoo," was propelled by Zionist propaganda. Why? The "official" name of it was "Search Engine Yahoo," and it rhymes with Netanyahu, the ex-Israeli Prime Minister, who is not over-loved by the Arabs.

PLAYING BRIDGE

The opening of the borders between Israel and Jordan in 1994 confronted Israel's Arab population with a new challenge and opportunity. For the first time, they could travel quite easily with their own cars to Jordan and meet their relatives, who had lived there since 1948. It was an eye-opening experience, which included a heavy dosage of stock-taking and comparing notes on every possible level.

Having lived in Jewish Israel, spoken Hebrew, and having had many partnerships with Israeli Jews, made the Israeli Arabs a strange entity in Jordanian eyes, to both those of Palestinian origin or of East Bank/Bedouin background.

The Anti-Normalization forces in Jordan played their role as well, slowing and quite effectively damaging many attempts to forge professional and commercial contacts between Jordan and Israel. Many Israeli Arabs were quick to realize that there was a problem and felt that they were uniquely qualified to try to bridge the gap, or to "play bridge," between Israel and Jordan, because of their intimate acquaintance with the Israeli mentality and because of their Arab/Palestinian origin.

These sincere attempts took many shapes and forms. Their main thrust and message was that they knew the Israelis and could explain to the Jordanians how the Israeli system worked, thus allaying most of the Jordanians' fears and suspicions.

Well, it was not that simple. Many Israeli Arabs, mainly in business and free professions, went, knowingly or unknowingly, through a process of Israelization (there is even a new noun to this effect in Arabic: Asralah), and it made them quite suspect by their brethren in Jordan. Their businesslike approach and a drive to cut a deal alarmed many Jordanians, some even suspecting that they were some kind of Israeli agents. To overcome these obstacles, some of them resorted to even more aggressive marketing methods, thus further estranging their target audiences.

All in all, it was quite frustrating, certainly to the Israeli Arabs, who really tried their best to "play bridge." I'm sure that each of them drew his or her own conclusions from this experience. The real blow occurred one day when a cynical Jordanian friend, who had witnessed some of these attempts, turned to me and remarked "*Yaaqub* (Jacob in Arabic), do they really believe that we need them to talk to you?"

THE POPULATION OF CAIRO (MIDDLE EASTERN STATISTICAL DATA)

Cairo is a bustling metropolis. Life basically never stops there. Shops and restaurants are open 20 hours per day and streets are crowded, even at midnight.

No one really knows what the population of Cairo is, since so many people live in unauthorized neighborhoods, even in the "City of the Dead," a huge, ancient cemetery.

Since I do not like black holes, I decided to try to find out. I knew an Egyptian businessman who was a native of Cairo, had lived there most of his life, and with whom we had working relations. One day, I asked him whether he, with all his background and field experience, would tell me what the population of Cairo was.

He responded by asking me what I meant. I replied that I had heard some confusing numbers and accounts in this respect. Some say that there are about 12 million; others say that there are14 million. Others even claim 16 million. There is another version that says actually there are 12 million, but during the day about 4 million flock in from the countryside and by the evening most of those return, *Inshallah*, back to the countryside. So, I asked which is the right number.

My Egyptian acquaintance looked at me for a long minute, with his sly eyes and then said: "*Ya Yaaqub* (Oh, Jacob), and if I'll tell, what can you do with it?"

I was taken aback for a moment, surprised by his response. He offered me another cup of coffee. Reflecting upon it later on, I realized that he was right. At a certain point and at certain circumstances, numbers lose their value.

REFUGEENESS: A SHORT ESSAY ON TERMINOLOGY

Some of the striking aspects of the Palestinian refugee problem are its terminology, its self-perceptions, and its addictions.

I myself am a son of uprooted people (I was born in 1948 in an occupied territory in Walbrzych, Lower Silesia, Poland, which was, until 1945, a German city called Waldenburg). I know that the first and the most urgent purpose of everyone involved is to end and shorten the transitional period of *Refugee-ness*, either by self action or through external efforts from whoever is available and willing to help.

The Palestinians, on the other hand, somehow took another course with the silent participation of their "hosting" Arab countries and their own leadership. They perpetuated it and, except for Jordan, they almost "froze" the frame.

The problem is that the world did not freeze and other refugee problems were solved, to a certain extent. I lived in India, which also witnessed huge refugee waves following the war with Pakistan in 1948. The Palestinian situation also did not freeze after 1948, despite the efforts to leave it as it was.

Every change resulted in coining another terminology, and anyone who wants to understand the complexities should familiarize himself with the following terms:

Refugees of 1948—Palestinians who left the territories which are now the State of Israel and settled mostly in refugee camps in Lebanon, Syria, Iraq, Egypt (Gaza Strip), and Jordan (West Bank and East Bank) following the war of 1948.

Refugees of 1967—Palestinians, who escaped from the West Bank to Jordan following the 1967 war. Some of them were genuine residents of the West Bank and some of them were 1948 refugees who lived in refugee camps in the West Bank. Some of them, from both groups, were in the East Bank of the Jordan in June 1967, and following the war, could not return to the West Bank. These are usually termed as displaced persons (*Nazihin* in Arabic).

Refugees of 1991 (from Kuwait)—This is a group of about 400,000 who were expelled by the Kuwaitis following the liberation of that country from the Iraqi occupation. They are regarded as Repatriates or '*Aidun*' (Returnees). This group is distinct from other refugees, because it is getting paid compensations for the property it lost in Kuwait and is being looked upon by other Palestinian refugees (1948,1967) as lucky, spoiled and different. Some of them were never refugees previously, since they came originally from cities and villages in the West Bank and moved to Kuwait during the 60's and 70's.

And what about the Arabs of Israel who stayed there following the war of 1948? Well, they total, nowadays, more than a million; they have about 10 members in the Israeli parliament (out of 120) and are citizens of the Jewish State. Seen for a few decades by their refugee brethren as cowards, Quislings, and collaborators with the Zionists, they also began coming of age. They call themselves "*Arabs of 48*," which may sound a little bit internet-ish. Recently, they inaugurated a website called *www.arabs48.org*

THE SECOND TEMPLE TREASURES

The Jews and the Israelis are perceived by most of the Arabs as rich, greedy, and cunning. This is a result of systematic exposure to demonization by the authorities and the lack of freedom to access information or literature. The strong U.S-Israeli relations just amplify what they have read already in *The Protocols of the Elders of Zion.*

A few weeks after opening the Embassy, in February 1995, I believe, I was approached by a Jordanian Bedouin who told me that he had an access to a cave near Madba (south of Amman near Mount Nebo), where there was a tremendous treasure of gold from the Second Temple. "It was offered already to the Americans for 500 million US dollars, but since the treasure is of significance to the Jews," he said that he was willing to sell the treasure to the Israelis. Of course, I referred him loudly to the Jordanian Antiquities Law and told him that if he knew of such a treasure, he should inform the Jordanian authorities. I even volunteered to put him in contact with the relevant agency.

Needless to say, he disappeared quite quickly.

A few weeks later, a Palestinian who was working in the commercial section of a Western Embassy visited me. I assumed that he wanted to find a job with us and to offer his expertise. Much to my surprise, he raised the story of the cave and the Second Temple gold. I repeated, loudly, our position. He disclosed to me that a friend, who dropped him at the Embassy, was in a car in the parking lot downstairs with samples of the treasure for me to see. I declined to go down.

A few days later, an Israeli contractor visited me and asked whether I could help him with a "sensitive national issue." He was offered the Second Temple treasures, but he "understood" that it would be complicated to get them out of Jordan and into Israel.

He asked whether it would be possible to transfer them in a diplomatic pouch. To add to his credibility, he whispered that he knew the Director of the Israeli Antiquities Authority. I told him that the meeting was over.

I can only assume that the Second Temple treasures are still buried safely in the cave near Madba.

THIS TIME I CAME WITH A PASSPORT

The Jordanian-Israeli relations since 1948 are full of tragedies, blood, and misunderstandings. During the 50's, there were many infiltrations from Jordan into Israel, many of them by armed Palestinians who came to steal and sabotage, sometimes even to kill. These infiltrations were countered by military retaliations by the I.D.F (Israeli Defense Forces). Some of these retaliatory actions were complicated and performed by top military units. A whole folklore and personality cult grew around some of the brave who lost their lives, either in military actions or trying to sneak into Petra in South Jordan.

Many Israelis participated during the 50's and 60's in actions behind the Jordanian enemy lines, some of them clandestine until today.

[This book is not a psychological study of the Israeli machismo, though it does deserve some serious examination.]

The Jordanians are a kind and very hospitable people. When they meet a foreigner/tourist, they will almost always ask where the person is from and whether it is his/her first visit to Jordan. Most of the foreigner/tourists will answer with a compliment about the beauty of the country, etc.

Not the Israelis! Encountering such a routine question, the Israeli machos will respond most of the time with a wide and victorious smile: "This is the first time I am visiting here with a passport and visa...."

My friend, Shalom Tourgeman, who was Second Secretary in the Embassy, once accompanied an Israeli Minister who was asked by his Jordanian counterpart whether it was his first visit to Jordan. His proud response was, "No. Last time, I was here with tanks."

VISA TO THE U.S.A.

The myth of far-reaching Jewish influence is deeply embedded in the minds of many people in the Middle East and elsewhere. Some obtained their knowledge through *The Protocols of the Elders of Zion.* The myth is that World Jewry and The State of Israel are harmonically coordinated and synchronized with a clear division of labor, both in Washington and in Moscow.

Since the Jews are always cunning, according to popular belief, there is no room for coincidence or mistakes. With everything being well coordinated and supervised, there is no margin for a "mistake" or "blunder" on the Israeli side! I hope that I do not breach the Israeli Civil Service Regulations, which do not allow a civil servant to disclose information which he obtained while discharging his duties, but we *DO* commit mistakes from time to time.

One of the well-established axioms in the Arab world is that the Jews/Israel control the White House (and the Kremlin as well, after the collapse of the U.S.S.R.) Start with Allen Greenspan, Madeline Albright, Dennis Ross, and, of course, Monica Lewinski.

One day, a very respected Jordanian phoned me and asked for an appointment to see me. In some of the cases, these meetings ended with the guest pulling a few passports from his pocket and asking me to help him obtain a visa to Israel/West Bank for his friends or relatives. In most of the cases, those people were perfectly eligible for a visa, unless there was a security problem. My intervention was basically unnecessary, except for the good feeling of my guest who felt that he had contacts in the Embassy. After a while, and with the natural increase of those requests, we found a way to fax to our acquaintances an appointment form in the Consular Section. So, when someone would call, we would try to find out whether he needed a visa, and then we would fax him the appropriate form.

One day, we got one of those calls. The caller, a senior government official, denied my secretary's inquiry that his call was about a visa and insisted on talking with me. When I picked the phone up and asked him what his request was, he said that he would rather not discuss it over the phone, but "face to face."

The next day, he showed up. We had coffee, and then he pulled out a few passports. I got "offended" and told him that we could have faxed the visa forms, since I remembered that his relatives traveled in the past to the West Bank and had the security clearance.

Much to my surprise, he responded that he needed my intervention with the U. S. Embassy Visa Section. When I responded that I may be a "big shot" in the Israeli Embassy, but I did not have any influence whatsoever with the American Embassy's Visa Section, he looked at me in disbelief and said, "What do you mean? You control the White House but cannot arrange a visa?!"

This reminds me of another case in one of our embassies in Eastern Europe in the mid- 90's.

One day, the Security Officer called the Ambassador and informed him that a high ranking official from the local Ministry of Foreign Affairs was at the gate and wanted to see him. That was strange because, according to diplomatic protocol, officials from the local Ministry of Foreign Affairs do not come to the Embassy, unless in a case of signing a condolences book or raising a toast after the presentation of credentials. It is the diplomats who visit the Ministries of Foreign Affairs. The second odd thing was that he didn't call for an appointment; he just showed up.

After verifying his identity, the high official was admitted and accompanied to the Ambassador's Office. Upon entering, he handed the Ambassador an envelope addressed to Mr. Charles Bronfman, a Canadian citizen who is owner of Seagram's distilleries and who is also the President of the World Jewish Congress (with headquarters in New York). He asked the Ambassador to forward it. Our Ambassador tried to explain patiently to the high-ranking emissary that he was the Ambassador of the State of Israel and Mr. Bronfman is a Canadian citizen, with forwarding addresses in Canada and the U.S.A.

The local official was taken slightly aback and, half offended, responded, "Come on, Excellency, do not play formalities with us, you and Bronfman are one company; you can forward it."

WARRIORS FOR JERUSALEM (A TRIBUTE TO DONALD NEFF)

The battle for Jerusalem in 1948 between the Israelis and the Arabs was a fierce one. The major force on the Arab side was the Arab Legion (the Jordanian Army). Among the Jordanian warriors was a young colonel of Circassian origin, Fawaz Maher Barmamet. Bulky and courageous, he gave a hard time to the Israeli forces, who were trying to break the siege on Jerusalem.

One of those who commanded the Israeli forces was a young Lt. Col. Yitzhak Rabin. In 1952, both of them studied at the British Staff College at Camberley and found out that they fought each other in 1948. They actually liked each other and appreciated each other's combat performance.

Upon return to Jordan, Fawaz Maher became Chief of Staff of the Army and later began a long diplomatic career as Ambassador to Taiwan, Iraq, Iran, and Turkey.

Yitzhak Rabin became Chief of Staff in 1965, and in 1969 he became Israel's Ambassador to the U.S.A. Later he became Prime Minister. They followed each other's careers, but it was not until early 1994, during one of Rabin's secret visits to the Royal Palace in Amman (before the signing of the Peace Agreement), that he dared to ask King Hussein about Fawaz Maher. King Hussein decided to surprise Rabin.

It was late at night and since Fawaz Maher's residence was about a five-minute drive from the Hashemiyyah Palace (where the meetings between the Jordanians and the Israelis were taking place), the King sent a driver to Fawaz Maher's residence and asked him to come to the Palace immediately.

What does one do, if the King asks him to come to the Palace? He goes.

As a faithful soldier, despite his frail health (he was already in his early seventies), he dressed up and went to the Palace to be surprised by the presence of his "old buddy."

The next time they met was on October 17, 1994, during the signing of the Peace Agreement in the Arava Valley.

One day early in 1995, the health of Fawaz Maher deteriorated, and his doctor thought that it would be a good idea to send him abroad for treatment, but no one was sure whether he would be able to make the long flight. Then, King Hussein suggested that they try Hadassah Hospital in Jerusalem and have him transported there by air. So, we coordinated the flight, with the Jordanian chopper being escorted by an Israeli one upon crossing the Jordan River. Fawaz Maher arrived incognito at Hadassah hospital.

It was Ambassador Shimon Shamir who arranged everything with the hospital and also informed Prime Minister Rabin about the new patient in the hospital. Prime Minister Rabin decided to visit the Fawaz Maher, but, unfortunately, while on the way to the hospital, another terrorist attack occurred in the city, with many wounded and, of course, journalists rushing to the hospital. There was no doubt Prime Minister Rabin's presence in the hospital would be noticed by the media, so, frustrated, he had to turn back. He returned the following week.

When Prime Minister Rabin was assassinated, we opened the Ambassador's residence for the acceptance of expressions of condolences. Ambassador Shamir was in Israel with King Hussein to attend the funeral, so I was in residence with the Ambassador's wife, Daniella, receiving the hundreds of Jordanians who came to offer their condolences and sympathy.

Among them were Fawaz Maher's wife, Um Ali, and his daughter. She told us that her husband sat at home crying and weeping at the "death of a courageous soldier and a good friend."

NOTE: See by comparison, the version of Mrs.Leah Rabin's book—Rabin, Leah: *Rabin, Our Life, His Legacy* (New York, 1997), pp.91-94.

Was There a Holocaust?

One of the main characteristics of the Arab-Israeli conflict is the tremendous gap of information about the "other." On the Israeli side, this is mainly a voluntary choice, and sometimes a failure of the system to encourage people to learn more about their neighbors. The situation on the Arab side is due to a lack of access to information. In other words, the nature and conduct of the authorities is such that access to free information is strictly controlled, and people who wish to make their own inquiries and try to gain such information, find their attempts aborted one way or another.

A very poignant point comes to my mind — The Holocaust. Being myself a "second-generation" of Holocaust survivors and a book collector, I was quite flabbergasted by the absence of any factual literature about this subject in Egypt and in Jordan. All that the Arab reader can find in these countries (and, I presume, that this is the case in the rest of the Arab World) is literature which claims that the Holocaust is a myth/ploy, invented by the Zionist movement to squeeze money from the Europeans and to justify the establishment of the State of Israel. Some books by Holocaust deniers were translated into Arabic. Our attempts, in the late 80's, to distribute in Egypt a book in Arabic about the Holocaust met fierce resistance from the authorities.

One day, in 1998, I was asked by a Palestinian friend with close contacts to the literary community in Amman, whether the Holocaust really happened. I, of course, became intrigued and said, "Yes." But also asked in return, "Why do you ask?"

His response was that he had an acquaintance with a playwright who intended to write something on the subject. I told my friend that my mother, who was still alive at that time, was herself a Holocaust survivor and was imprisoned in Auschwitz. It was a closer shot than he expected when he first asked, and, upon his request for further details, I added that my mother had tattooed on her left arm the famous prisoner's serial number. He found it quite unbelievable, and to convince him, I volunteered to take a photo of it the next time I visited my parents. In about two weeks' time, I came back with a photo depicting my mother with her *A-26368* number. He was quite amazed and found it difficult to believe. He took the photo with him. So far, I have not seen that any use was made of it.

This story has another personal twist. Three years later, in the summer of 2001, I met, at a garden party in Atlanta, Georgia, a Jewish lady, who had an *A-27373* number tattooed on her arm. It occurred to me that from the proximity of the numbers that she might have been on the same transport train as my mother, and probably originated from the same city. I asked her gently, "Excuse me, are you by any chance from Krakow?" She, in disbelief, responded, "Yes."*

*An article about this was published in *The Atlanta Journal* on July 26, 2001.

WE'VE NEVER HAD ISRAELIS OR JEWS HERE BEFORE

When I arrived in Amman in December 1994, I didn't think I'd stay there for more than a month. It so happened that at a certain stage, we decided to stay there for a whole diplomatic tenure. That meant that our children, at the elementary and high school levels, had to find schooling in Amman.

I started looking around and found out that there was an American Community School, like in almost any other major city abroad. This school had an interesting history, since it was closed for a few months during the Gulf War in 1991. More than half of its students were Arab, either children of Arabs who had lived previously in the West or of mixed marriages (where one of the parents is from the West).

So, one day I made my way to the Superintendent of that school. He was a very experienced American educator and administrator. I gladly informed him that next year he would have some Israeli students in his school.

The smiling and easy going Superintendent turned very serious and responded: "Oh, Mr. Rosen, it might be slightly touchy. We have never had Israeli or Jewish kids here in the past."

He probably knew what he was talking about, since many of the Arab children in the school were of Palestinian background. I did not loose my cool and responded that our children had some "breakthrough experiences"—having been the first Israeli children in the American Embassy School in New Delhi, India. They had also studied in the Cairo American College, so they could handle new environments and were used to studying with Arab children.

The Superintendent relaxed after hearing my soothing statement and suggested that I bring the children, on the earliest possible occasion, to Amman for an orientation tour of the school.

Have I already mentioned that this Superintendent was experienced? Yes, he was. In April 1995, our three children came to visit the school. Each respective class formed a "welcome committee," composed of three students who stayed with our children the whole day, enabling them to see and meet their future co-eds.

It worked! Our children had a very interesting experience and made many, many Arab friends. Our oldest son, Etai, is the first Israeli to graduate from high school in Jordan, and all our children continue corresponding with their friends through the Internet.

Thank you, Dr. Gary Duckett, for your wisdom and experience. Thank you *Yahoo!* and *Hotmail* for keeping those friendships alive.

WE KNOW BETTER; WE'LL TEACH YOU

Reflecting upon the causes of discomfort and uneasiness which the Arabs feel towards the Americans and Israelis, one may add also the approach they radiate towards the Arabs, sometimes without even saying a word. The American and Israeli approach (including that of Israeli Arabs who have gone through a process of "*Israelization*") is that we belong to the developed world, which has achieved so much, and we are willing or obliged to share with "them" our advantages. While this is basically right, it is the tone and the body language which sometimes make this attitude a problem.

While the Arab culture and behavior tend to pay a lot of attention and time to hospitality and small talk, the Americans and, to a lesser degree the Israelis, are much more time and business oriented. They come with timetables, blueprints, deadlines and a concept that time is money and that we have to keep to a schedule. The Arabs, on the other hand, have survived many centuries with a different attitude, and they even managed to build an impressive civilization, at a time when Europe was deep in the Dark Ages and America was still Indian.

One day we had a joint meeting with the Jordanians in the Jordan River Crossing (Sheikh Hussein), which is the Northern border crossing between Jordan and Israel. The Japanese Government donated the money to build a four-lane bridge over the Jordan River. We came to discuss the final stages of the construction. For a variety of reasons, the contractor was a Jordanian company. A Jordanian Military Liaison Officer who, after the meeting, offered the Israelis the opportunity to speak with the Jordanian construction team, accompanied us.

One Israeli engineer accepted the offer, and, down in the mud, we stepped under the bridge. There stood a man in rubber boots and a sweater, who seemed to be the man in charge. The Jordanian Liaison Officer indicated to the Israeli engineer that this was his counterpart and led them to shake hands. The Israeli engineer, while shaking the Jordanian's hand, turned to the Liaison Officer and asked if the engineer spoke English. The Jordanian, upon hearing this indirect question, answered calmly: "Yes, I speak English."

Having overcome this hurdle, the Israeli started asking questions about the ratio of cement and sand, which they used for the construction of the bridge. The Jordanian replied (in a better English than that of the Israeli's) that they used 400 kg of cement per tonne. This was, of course, the straw, which "broke" the Israeli macho. The Israeli responded immediately and triumphantly saying: "We use 500 kg per tonne."

I almost buried myself in the mud. It was so typical and so embarrassing. It was especially painful because the Israeli engineer was a good man and certainly had no wish or intention to offend his Jordanian counterpart.

WHERE IS AMMAN?

Our son, Etai, studied in the American Community School in Amman. At the age of 17, he was called up, like any other Israeli citizen, to register at the Military Recruitment Office in Jerusalem to get medical check ups, interviews, etc. Since Jerusalem is not far from Amman (about two hours by car), he took a day off from school and went to Jerusalem "to be processed."

He showed up, like hundreds of others of his peers, at the Jerusalem Military Recruitment Office. When his turn came, he presented himself to the female military clerk, who routinely, even without looking at him, tried to verify/fill-in his personal details.

"Are you Etai Rosen?" she asked.

"Yes," he responded.

"Where do you live?" she continued.

"In Amman," he said.

"Where is Amman?" she inquired, having apparently never heard of such a location before.

"It is not far from Jericho," my son clarified.

"Is it a *moshav* or a *kibbutz*?" she asked.*

*Note: *Moshav* and *Kibbutz* are two kinds of unique cooperative agricultural settlements for which Israel became famous.

WHERE DID YOU SLEEP LAST NIGHT?

Honor is one of the main keys to understanding the Arab society, providing of course, that we agree on a definition of that honor. Whatever the agreed upon definition might be, it is elementary for the very survival in one's social environment. While in the Western society, one may survive quite well even if he is not respected and honored, this is not the case in the Arab society, where the family's/clan's financial and physical support and backing are indispensable.

Honor requires that one does not openly raise a private problem or issue, including not even admitting that there is one. One does not discuss sex or even dating (wherever it exists). Discussing "relations" is also taboo, to a degree. Asking a woman about acquaintances with males may be interpreted as doubting her integrity and purity or, in other words, questioning her honor.

When Israel's "El-Al" airlines started flying to Amman, along with it came its famous/notorious security procedures.

Considered to be the best in the world, it bases its security on human, rather than on technical, screening. These procedures include engaging the passenger in a conversation and trying to find out more about him, rather than what is in the luggage he carries. The questions are intrusive, repetitive and are interpreted, sometimes, as both stupid and casting doubt on the integrity and honor of the passenger.

Therefore, you can imagine what the reaction of a Muslim female from a traditional background might be to a "standard" question about who her friends are or where she slept last night. I will relieve you from describing some of the angry telephone calls we got in the Embassy from very insulted Jordanians about our abrasive questions and our casting of doubts on the purity and the dignity of female members of their families.

THE SANDWICH TOURISM

The Peace Agreement between Jordan and Israel caught the Jordanian public by surprise. They were unprepared for it. No one really "warned" them that peace was in the cards. The rapid pace of events, from the meeting between King Hussein and Yitzhak Rabin in the White House in July 1994, until the signing of the Peace Agreement in October 1994, was maddening to them.

Unlike the Egyptians, who had a two-year interval between Sadat's visit to Jerusalem in 1977 and the signing of the Peace Agreement with Israel, the Jordanians had no more than three months to digest the change.

Of course, people respected King Hussein's decision, but they had plenty of questions and needed some clarifications. The government's machinery apparently never thought of a plan or scheme of how to prepare the public for such a change. The quick pace, of course, did not help. What was somehow conveyed to the public sounded, it appeared, that "everything was going to be O.K. now. We are going to have a lot of investments; our economy will improve, and unemployment will disappear."

President Clinton's speech to the Jordanian Parliament prior to the signing of the Peace Agreement, gave a rise to the hope that the U. S. would pump huge amounts of dollars into Jordan (Egypt received, since 1980, about $2 billion annually in American aid). Those expectations were, of course, unrealistic. The Democrats lost their majority on Capitol Hill in the elections a few weeks later, and, in any case, Jordan had only 4 million inhabitants and not 60 million like Egypt had. So even if President Clinton had kept his promise, Jordan would have gotten only a portion of what Egypt was receiving.

Until 1994, Jordan had no practical experience in dealing with investments from abroad, at least not in an institutional manner. Some individuals who worked in the Gulf or Saudi Arabia may have come back with savings and bought property or invested it in a family business, but nothing beyond that.

The public thought that American investors would flock to Jordan and "cover" it with investments. Of course, that was very unrealistic. American investors are very careful and require a lot of answers and data before making any operational decisions. Even people who came and wanted to invest struggled with getting reliable economic data or getting guarantees about basic infrastructures, such as telephone lines, market research, etc.

The Jordanian business community, both the commercial and the industrial, many of whose members were of Palestinian origin, had to struggle to maintain contacts with Iraq, which was subject to severe economic sanctions imposed by the U.N. They were also hesitant about economic contacts with Israel, both for political reasons and out of fear that the Israeli economic drive would engulf them and would push them out of business.

Needless to say, no new jobs in the countryside emerged (except for the industrial zone in Irbid called *[Q.I.Z.] Qualified Industrial Zone*). The Peace Agreement didn't create jobs in Ramtha, Zarqa, Al Karak, or Ma'an. The only change was in tourism, when Israelis started visiting Jordan in growing numbers. This was also not simple. Jordan has wonderful archeological and religious sights, but almost no recreational facilities for tourists with children. Most of the Israelis wanted to see Petra and were curious about Amman, Jarash (20 miles north of Amman), or Mount Nebo.

All in all, no more than two nights (three days) were spent in Jordan. Since most of the Israeli tourists came by bus, and since some of them observed Jewish dietary laws, they would bring sandwiches with them or cans of kosher food, which was not available in Amman. Most the Israelis came with organized tours (Israeli Arabs stayed mostly at their relatives' homes, whenever possible). Therefore, the tourism industry, souvenir shops, and restaurants did not see a terrific boom in their businesses.

Soon we started hearing complaints from the Jordanians about the "Sandwich Tourists." The main complaint: the Israelis brought their sandwiches from Israel, visited only archeological sights and did not spend money in Jordan. The fact that the entry ticket to Petra cost about US$40 was conveniently forgotten. Cities and areas without archeological sites did not see tourists, nor jobs at all.

Very quickly, their motto was: "We do not see the fruits of peace."

THE EXPERTS

The establishment of relations between Israel and Jordan gave a rise to a new group: *The Experts*. Many Israeli businesses and institutions were eager to explore the potential of the Jordanian market and were desperately looking for experts who knew Jordan or knew people who knew Jordanians. There was such a contingent—ex-Israeli Civil and Military Administration officers who, since 1967, were in charge of the West Bank and the Gaza Strip and who knew many Palestinians with family or business connections in Jordan.

What could have been better: a group of experienced people with "Arabist background," some of them even decorated military figures, who knew Palestinians with business experience and contacts in Jordan? There was nothing there which could have gone wrong, was there? Well, not exactly. We all learned gradually and the hard way.

The first warning signs were telephone calls from offices of Israeli Mayors who were promised by their *Experts* that they would fix for them an appointment in the Royal Place. "The appointments were fixed," we were told, "but," so went the argument, "the Royal Palace asked to formalize it with a letter from the Israeli Embassy." Our attempts to find out what the purpose of those meetings was, and at what level, didn't get us very far. What we managed to reconstruct was that some Palestinians with whom they were in touch, convinced them that they could arrange such an appointment.

After a while the experts started showing up in Amman in person. We met some of them. Their reaction to their first encounter with Amman was total surprise and astonishment. Living under the impression that Amman was probably and upgraded version of *Nablus* or *Hebron* they discovered a civilized modern city with four lane boulevards, traffic lights and extreme cleanliness. Time and again we were asked how Amman was so clean and functional. I would sometimes answer teasingly that it was an Arab city that was not "run" by an Israeli military governor.

Then came the harder part. The experts came to do business and establish contacts. Some of them came accompanied by their Palestinian acquaintances and some of them came alone, equipped with the telephone numbers of the Jordanians they intended to meet. Here came "lesson #2" — some Jordanians wouldn't agree to meet them. This was very painful to digest, especially for ex-military governors and deputy governors who could, in their "hey days," summon almost anyone to their offices. Suddenly, a Jordanian says "No" to you and there is nothing you can do about it. Well, almost nothing. As a last resort some of them came to the Israeli Embassy and asked for advice and guidance. Together we tried to reconstruct what they had done so far and to analyze what, and at which stage, went wrong.

It was a heart breaking experience in many cases. Very experienced and mature people who were confident that they "knew the Arabs" discovered to their dismay that experience and knowledge were also a matter of geography. What was a solid asset in the West Bank was not applicable in Jordan.

There were, of course, a few exceptions and success stories. The key to their success was not business entrepreneurship, but the wisdom to realize that they were not a military governor any more and that they had better listen rather than lecture. Arabs are eager to learn. They hate to be taught. Especially by Israelis.

A TEMPORARY CAR

Bureaucracies like routine. Bureaucracies do not like changes. Bureaucracies, wherever they reside, hate situations which will create precedents.

The Peace Agreement between Jordan and Israel facilitated the passage of cars from country to country. At a certain stage we also allowed entry of cars from Oman and Qatar where Israel had opened liaison offices.

One day a Jordanian businessman whom I knew called me and inquired whether his friend who resided in the United Arab Emirates (U.A.E.), but was a holder of a Jordanian passport, could obtain a visa to Israel. I responded that he could. There was a slight problem since we couldn't see his passport. Nevertheless we began the process based on photocopies which he faxed to us.

When he finally arrived in Amman we granted him the visa, and he and his Jordanian friend headed to the border crossing, driving his car with U.A.E. license plates. They checked out the car at the Jordanian customs and crossed to the Israeli side. After completing the immigration procedures, they were informed by the Israeli customs personnel that they couldn't bring the car to Israel.

"Why?" they asked, surprised.

"U.A.E. is an enemy country, and the Israeli law does not permit the entry of cars from enemy states."

The tourists tried to argue that the U.A.E. was not an enemy and that in any case if there was any suspicion about the car it could be checked thoroughly, "Israeli style."

The customs people persisted in their refusal. After a while the Jordanian told his friend that he thought that there was no chance to convince the Israelis and advised him to return the car to the Jordanian side. He returned it, and then crossed back to Israel. They managed their way around Israel with taxis and rental cars. All in all they had a good time but were frustrated by the Israeli refusal to let the U.A.E. car come in.

Upon returning to Jordan, the Jordanian businessman asked to see me and told me the story. He basically reprimanded me for our shortsightedness. "I have friends in the U.A.E. who have a lot of money which they are willing to spend in Israel. Your refusal was stupid." Trying to make a point he continued: "I thought that the Jews were clever people. What do you want from the poor car? It was manufactured in the United States, and by sheer chance bears U.A.E. license plates. You want to check the car? Check it! Why do you try to keep away rich Arab tourists who are willing to visit Israel?"

His arguments were logical and made sense. So I decided to try to look into what the problem was. What I found was amazing: the ban on the U.A.E. car stemmed from a British regulation that was introduced in Mandatory Palestine during WWII to prevent imports from enemy countries. The regulation had not been abolished since.

I raised the issue with several departments in the Ministry of Foreign Affairs in Jerusalem, and pointed to the potential tourism from the Gulf States if we allowed cars from those states to enter Israel. A young lawyer at the legal division of the Ministry pointed out that the regulation was against imports from enemy countries, but in our case it was a "temporary import" since by the end of the tour, the car went back and is being "exported."

It was a very solid argument and was accepted by the Israeli customs. The regulation is still valid, but temporary is temporary.

INDEX

ABOUT THE AUTHOR

Born in Poland in 1948. His family immigrated to Israel in 1957. Served in the Israeli Defense Forces from 1966 to 1969. Attended the Hebrew University in Jerusalem and received a B.A. degree in Middle Eastern Studies in 1972.

Joined the Israeli Ministry of Foreign Affairs in 1973. Served since in The Hague, London, New York, Cairo and New Delhi. In December 1994 opened the Israeli Embassy in Amman, Jordan and served there as charge d'affaires until the arrival of the Ambassador and continued his post in Amman as Deputy Chief of Mission until July 2000 when he was appointed Consul General of Israel in Atlanta, Georgia.

In November 2002, he took up the post of Political Advisor for International Affairs to the Mayor of Jerusalem. Jacob is married to Annette. They are parents of two sons and a daughter. Is fluent in Polish, Dutch, English, Arabic and Hebrew and understands Russian,French, German and Yiddish. He is an avid collector of books on "Lawrence of Arabia."

www.ingramcontent.com/pod-product-compliance
Lightning Source LLC
Jackson TN
JSHW021129071225
95310JS00001B/126